MW01502506

BLEEDING BETWEEN THE LINES

ELIOT ASINOF

BLEEDING : BETWEEN THE " " * LINES

Holt, Rinehart and Winston   New York

Published by Holt, Rinehart and Winston, 383 Madison Avenue,
New York, New York 10017.
Published simultaneously in Canada by Holt, Rinehart and Winston of
Canada, Limited.

Library of Congress Cataloging in Publication Data
Asinof, Eliot, 1919–
Bleeding between the lines.
1. Talent Associates.   2. Asinof, Eliot, 1919–   3. Susskind, David, 1920–
4. Copyright–Broadcasting rights–United States.
5. Television industry–United States.   6. Asinof, Eliot, 1919–
7. Chicago. Baseball club (American League)   8. World Series (Baseball)
I. Title.
KF228. T28A85   343'.73'078   78-14181
ISBN 0-03-047536-8

FIRST EDITION

DESIGNER: *Joy Chu*
Printed in the United States of America
10 9 8 7 6 5 4 3 2 1

*One last tip of the hat to the memory of
Oscar "Happy" Felsch—and a belated salute
of gratitude to Vance Bourjaily*

I was ruined twice in my life. Once when I lost a lawsuit, and once when I won one.

—Voltaire

BOOK ONE

"When I used to read fairy tales, I fancied that kind of thing never happened, and now here I am in the middle of one!"

—*Lewis Carroll,*
Alice's Adventures in Wonderland

1.

Let's begin with the ringing of my doorbell. It's a warm, humid afternoon in June 1976, and I'm finishing up work for the day. Though I expect no one, I go to the door with a Pavlovian sense of anticipation, having once opened that door to an exquisite girl who breathlessly asked if she might visit my bedroom which, she claimed, was the site of her conception. Another time, my son surprised me after a long hitchhiking trip across the country. Nor am I one to peer through the peephole or use the protective chain, for any such precautions would adulterate the pleasure of surprise. Whoever it is, let the unseen visitor face my joy head-on.

On this afternoon, then, I fling open the door to a tall, sandy-haired man in his mid-forties. A stranger in a plaid shirt and worn chino slacks, with several ball-point pens clipped to his shirt pocket, his hands clasped mysteriously behind his back.

I do my best to conceal my disappointment.

"Eliot Asinof?" he asks, the hint of a smile twinkling in his eyes.

"Yes?" I reply, and the smile spreads across his face, accompanied by an exaggerated sigh of relief, like one who had just found a long-lost brother.

"Been trying to get you for days," he says, suddenly exposing his hands, one of which thrusts a set of folded papers under my nose.

"What!" I cry out, and though I have never experienced this moment before, I immediately recognize a summons to do battle with the law.

"A legal complaint," he explains. "From Talent Associates."

No doubt he's read it through a dozen times as he sat waiting for me in the lobby.

Talent Associates, Ltd., is David Susskind's television and film production company. Since I've been in a protracted, unresolved negotiation with him, I suppose I should not be surprised. But I am.

What could possibly justify a lawsuit?

"Sorry 'bout this." He continues to twinkle as though this moment is his reward for all the waiting. "But you sure got trouble, pal."

I stare at him, wondering how he could justify such a gleeful manner when he claims such sympathy. He continues to stand there, waiting for me to make the next move. What am I supposed to do, tip him? I fumble with the papers, reluctant to open them, certainly not there in the doorway any more than I'd read a love letter in the presence of a mailman.

"Yeah . . . well, thanks," I say, and like a host with a departing guest, I wait for the elevator with him.

"Have a good day, mister . . . ha, ha," he says, casting his eyes for a parting caress at the papers in my hand.

"Ha, ha." I share the whimsy, a genial host right to the end. I even wave good-bye with the papers themselves as the elevator door finally closes on him, a stylish gesture if there ever was one.

Inside, the mood changes. Immediately, I feel betrayed. Sensing an oncoming wave of anxiety, I quickly toss the hostile papers on the kitchen table, turn to the refrigerator for the ice-cube tray and the start of a tall Scotch and soda—a refreshing pop to stall the inevitable confrontation with absurdity. I even return the whisky bottle to the cabinet, though I know I am going to work on it again. Drink in hand, I cross to the living-room window and a familiar view of the ailanthus tree in the courtyard below, where a large gray cat stretches, working its claws against the bark. I start on my drink, but a room away, those papers are screaming for attention. I feel foolish, like one who tries to hold his breath forever.

With the resignation of a condemned man walking to the hangman's scaffold, I finally unfold the papers, hearing my stomach complain as my eyes take in the bad news.

Page 1 is, in itself, enough to set any reasonable man's skin bristling.

SUPREME COURT OF THE STATE OF NEW YORK
COUNTY OF NEW YORK

-- X

TALENT ASSOCIATES LTD,

                                                    Plaintiff,

                                                                        COMPLAINT

            -against-

ELIOT ASINOF,

                                                    Defendant.

-- X

One does not have to be a graphic artist to appreciate that ludicrous tableau. The spacing, the indentations, the upper case plus underlining of the word COMPLAINT, the dashes surrounding the word -against-. It sets the tone for the pomp and gibberish to follow, four absurd pages dominated by such stuffy phrases as "upon information and belief," "by reason of the foregoing," "pursuant to the heretofore alleged agreements . . . ," all building to a grand finale that I expect to cherish for all time:

The Bottom Line, as they say, is that Eliot Asinof, Defendant, is being sued for a total of $1,750,000.

Naturally, I break out laughing.

A million and three-quarters, to put it mildly, is a bit more than I make in an average year. It crosses my mind that I might not find it nearly as funny if the suit were for a mere $10,000, a far more frightening figure. Frightening, yes, but not flattering. The way I see it, anything over a "mill" puts me in extremely distinguished company. I begin thinking I might even hold a press conference.

I refill my glass, a buttress for rereading the COMPLAINT, which I find even more preposterous on the second go-round, the details of which the reader will be spared until a more appropriate time. Suffice to say, at this point, it relates to a book of mine, *Eight Men Out,* about the Black Sox Scandal of 1919, wherein eight baseball players on the Chicago White Sox conspired with gamblers to fix the World Series. As for the charges against me, there is, I am convinced as I stand there with my Scotch, absolutely no basis to justify the action. Susskind would have to be acting upon *mis*information and *false* belief, and all the whereases and by-reason-of-the-foregoings are rooted in a bouquet of distortions.

Indeed, with a little help from my drink, I achieve a stirring moment of clarity: the truth is, it is not Susskind who should be suing me, but I who should be suing Susskind!

Sure. Ha, ha.

Having scaled that summit, I toss the COMPLAINT into the trash can and take my drink back to my study. The whole thing is just a bloody farce. He cannot really be serious about suing me. It's just something he has to do to cover the breakdown in our negotiations. Of course, I remember his phone call *threatening* to sue me, but I would never have believed it was anything but a tactic.

Or am I deluding myself?

After all, that isn't a threatening phone call, it's a legal document with the SUPREME COURT OF THE STATE OF NEW YORK as its authority, whatever that means. This is something I *have* to respond to, a process I must participate in.

By Christ, I'm going to have to hire a lawyer!

That grotesque thought sinks in, curdling my stomach. Not that I don't have friends who are lawyers, fine people, stand-up citizens. It's what happens when they practice that galls me. I begin to absorb the gruesome implications, the expenditures of time and money to fight a legal battle in which victory is merely the absence of defeat. It would be like kissing your ugly sister, or so they say in the jock world after battling to a draw. The best I can possibly win is the right to keep a gargantuan sum of money I don't even have.

Ha, ha, the man said.

I can already picture my friends going along with the joke. Ha, ha, boy are you getting screwed—that sort of thing. They wouldn't laugh if I broke my arm, and neither would I, but I can't help feeling that Susskind is going to hurt me a lot more.

I begin to panic. I grab the phone as if it were Susskind's throat, dial the familiar PL 3-1030, barely able to wait until that smiling switchboard voice declares herself. "Good afternoon, Talent Associates . . ."

"David Susskind, please." The "please" sounding more like "goddamnit!" When I reach his secretary, I am all but spitting bullets.

"Tell David I want to talk to him!"

"Certainly, Eliot," she replies, her voice tinkling like a Christmas sleigh bell, as though she knows all and can't wait to overhear the confrontation.

But Susskind is no fool. He keeps me waiting for thirty seconds, a minute, maybe more, stuffing my coming words deep into my throat. I try to contain my fury, to give him the best of me as well as the worst, but time quickly erodes my patience. When I hear his phone come alive, his voice is impatient, irritating: "Yes, Eliot, what is it?", and I am totally stumped. My mind, the bright, quicksilver mechanism that represents me in public, turns blank, impotent in fury. All I can do is hang up, viciously slamming the phone to its cradle, crying out "Shit!" in a wail of pain.

Ha, ha, I can still hear the man laughing.

My head is ringing and I am sweating beyond belief. For want of a better action, I make myself another drink, as slowly and deliberately as I am capable of moving. I sit, concentrating like a yogi to temper my furious pulse, knowing full well I haven't a chance. Every thought exacerbates the pressure. There's even a familiar feel to the torment, a sort of sinister déjà vu, a sweeping overall what-did-you-expect sort of reaction, like a professional ballplayer getting beaned, or a politician getting caught with his hand in the till, or a call girl catching a dose of clap.

Occupational hazards, right?

The point is, I'm a writer. Nobody forced me into it. And though I suffered through all the usual torments to become one, nowhere was it written that anything good or rewarding had to come of it. Quite the contrary, as any writer can tell you, it's a brutal struggle against colossal odds. A writer has to love the drama of it. He has to know how to feed on disaster, especially his own. He's got to see life as a wild flailing at windmills—and resist going bananas in the process.

Though I know all that, I am not prepared for what I now have to face. I see this monster looming over me and I tremble at the consequences. After all, it is more than a brouhaha between Susskind and me that has somehow gotten out of hand. It is the sort of crisis that can sum up your life for you. You're in it because that's the kind of person you are, however crazy it might seem. Deep in your gut you know this is no fluke. I suppose this is what jarred me so. Did it all come down to this absolutely idiotic confrontation?

I can tell you, it's a story of such deeply compounding absurdities that, by comparison, Alice's trip through Wonderland was a picnic as well as a tea party.

2.

When you appear in the sunny-bright offices of Paul, Weiss, Rifkind, Wharton, & Garrison in what seems like half the floor space in the glassy skyscraper at 345 Park Avenue, you are immediately conscious of enormous power. You tell yourself, this is where the Big Boys come to make their moves, and you pass through the spacious halls from floor to floor expecting to bump into cabinet ministers, chairmen of multinational-conglomerate boards, multimillionaire philanthropists, superstars of the entertainment world, perhaps even a king or two.

There was no question but that this was where I belonged.

When you get into legal trouble, you go to legal power. Everyone told me that.

"Find the biggest lawyer in New York!" they said.

"But I can't afford it," I'd protested.

"With one million, seven hundred and fifty thousand dollars at stake, you can't afford not to!" came the reply.

So the attorney was Edward N. Costikyan, distinguished partner of this celebrated law firm. A very special man, I was told. Extremely bright. Mind like a steel trap. A tiger in court. A real power lawyer who knew everyone.

He even knew *me*.

What's more, when he'd heard about my problems, he'd indicated considerable sympathy. And though he must have been fully aware that I did not have the kind of money his clients generally paid for his services, he was kind enough to welcome my visit.

He was a small man, but he showed none of the conventional complexes, Napoleonic or otherwise. He didn't even wear elevated shoes. Barely a week before, he had been mugged by two tough blacks. Sensibly enough, he had turned over his wallet to them, but when they decided to rough him up as well, he exploded, tearing into them both with a fury he did not know he had. They put him into the hospital for a few days, but he emerged the better for it all. I liked him. He was a man who laughed rarely but well. One would even describe his round, bespectacled face as an honest one, not at all bad for a lawyer who had also made some points as a politician.

"I hate these lawsuits," he said for openers.

Conundrum: Why is it almost impossible to find a lawyer who has a kind word to say about lawsuits, yet easy to find one who will take the case—on either side?

I would muse on that paradox, recalling John Dos Passos's reflection on Andrew Carnegie, the millionaire philanthropist who "was a dedicated man of peace—except in time of war."

I had a few well-mauled maxims of my own:

"What would happen if they had a lawsuit and nobody came?"

"All's fair in love and litigation."

"Ye shall hear of suits and rumors of suits: see that ye be not troubled, for . . . the end is not yet."

"Mankind must put an end to lawsuits, or lawsuits will put an end to mankind."

As for me, I'd come prepared for war, having put all the documents and notes together. I was ready with an ironclad defense, by God, for I had no intention of allowing David Susskind to walk away with my last million and three-quarters. I had always been

9

known as a tightwad and I was not going to allow such a distinguished reputation to go by the boards.

As I saw it, the case was all a matter of details. My lawyer had to be informed of details. He must see not only the facts but the nuances. Facts, after all, were a dime a dozen. Anyone could think up facts in support of their position. It was the nuances that supplied the meat of the real truth. I had to feed my lawyer the nuances behind the facts.

"Just tell me the facts," Costikyan said.

It all began about a year and a half ago. In the winter of 1975, I was finishing work on a book (*The Fox Is Crazy Too*) about a picaresque character named Garrett Brock Trapnell, a man who had enjoyed an enormously successful criminal career after constantly beating the courts by way of the Insanity Ruling. In the midst of such creative involvements, I received a phone call from David Susskind.

"Eliot . . . I want to buy *Eight Men Out.*"

No beating around the bush, no let's-talk-about-the-possibilities. He was ready to make a deal.

I was about to explain that it was impossible at this time, but he was assuming his most positive posture.

"I was with Herb Schmerz in Florida [Schmerz was Mobil Oil vice-president in charge of media] . . . he pulled your book off the shelf and said to me: '*Eight Men Out* is the finest sports book ever written. It should make a great television film.' "

"There are problems, David . . ."

He seemed not to hear this.

"Come down this afternoon," he said, "about three."

His organization, Talent Associates, Ltd., had moved since last I had seen him. From 444 Madison to 747 Third Avenue: a towering new office building with a unique wooden porch in the street, replete with flowerpots and director's chairs, the famed Joe and Rose's steak house beside it. TA was high on the thirty-third floor, its sole occupant, and the elevator opened on a spacious silvery-walled lobby that shimmered in the light, balanced with contrasting gray, white, and dark-brown furnishings. The room appeared to curl around me. No sharp edges anywhere. The entire reception area was without a corner! The unobtrusive reception desk was a half-moon with a sleek, low-slung switchboard. Above it, two huge glass bowls of light shone like full moons. The white shag rug was round, as was the coffee table and the side table adjacent to chrome chairs. Even the doorjambs and entrances to inner offices were curled. Remembering that old mock song "Go into the Round House, Nellie, he can't corner you there!" I speculated on whether this was designed to induce a comparable security.

There was only one small sign to identify the premises—a silvery stainless-steel plate hardly four inches tall, reading: TALENT ASSOCI-ATES, LTD. On the other wall areas there were photographs of Susskind's more prestigious productions: Sir Laurence Olivier in "The Moon and Sixpence," Sir John Gielgud in "The Browning Version," George C. Scott in "Death of a Salesman," Hal Holbrook's "Mark Twain Tonight!" And, as I moved into David's inner office, I noted a half-dozen more.

Susskind's office seemed more like a millionaire's study than a place of business, boasting a spectacular north-south see-through view of Manhattan. There were two davenports cornering a large coffee table; oriental rugs, a huge ottoman, and a luxurious Eames chair. A bookcase served as a room divider, and David's desk backed into the south window. In the main body of the room, tables were stacked high with books and screenplays, pictures of David's family, a few choice objets d'art. For it all, it did not seem cluttered—merely busy.

Indeed, it was the mark of David's success over the years. He had come out of Harvard, class of '42, served in the navy in communications, then worked as a press agent at Warner Brothers, went off on his own as a talent agent, and finally formed his own production company. "A young man in a hurry, a walking thesaurus, a seeker of prominence . . ." Jack Gould, once television critic of *The New York Times*, described him. He became the indomitable personality on his famous talk show "Open End," leading discussions on every conceivable current issue, seldom missing a chance to express his own opinions, going one-on-one in political debates with such celebrated figures as Nelson Rockefeller, Richard Nixon, Harry Truman. No one was too big for him, not even Nikita Khrushchev, at the time the most powerful man in the world.

As a producer, he was persistently responsible for the best shows on television. Almost alone among his colleagues, his history did not include pandering to the trash that networks seemed so eager to air. Above all, he refused to deal with violent themes.

I had written several television dramas and documentaries for Talent Associates over the years and was favorably impressed by the maturity of their approach—especially after working in Hollywood for five years.

Susskind had the best taste in town, a judgment I could doubly enjoy making since I was there, sitting in his office.

"There is no question that I'm finally going to make this film," David repeated.

The word *finally* was not without validity. Fifteen years earlier, we had met to discuss the possibility of a ninety-minute television dramatization of the Black Sox Scandal for the "Dupont Show of the Month." I was hired to research the incident, then write an outline of the action sufficient to convince the sponsors that such a show was feasible. For this, I was given two weeks, with a letter of agreement to pay me $1,000 for my efforts.

I went at it like a kid who had just found a dollar bill in front of a candy store. As it turned out, however, I'd hardly gotten in the door when Ford Frick, commissioner of baseball, determined that any such exposé of the scandal would "not be in the best interests of baseball" and convinced the Dupont people to cancel the production.

So it ended. The kid was thrown out of the candy store with barely a taste of the goodies. But not without whetting my appetite, for what became terribly apparent was the extraordinary scope and significance of the incident, infinitely more complex than anyone could even begin to grasp in a week's research. Indeed, when I took it on for a book, I needed almost two years to make sense of it.

Now, in 1975, David recognized its timeliness. The Black Sox Scandal, with its venality and corruption, its insidious betrayals and hypocritical cover-ups, its "story of cheaters cheating cheaters," as one of the characters had described it, was a historical replica of the more recent scandal that began at Watergate.

Unfortunately, however, I was there to bring him the bad news.

"I'm sorry, David," I said, "but I don't own the rights. They're under option."

Though that option had another fifteen months to run, the news wasn't all bad, I explained. As I saw it, they were not making progress and might very well want to sell the rights back to me.

Susskind was encouraged by that. "There's really no way *anyone* can make this for theatrical release. It's strictly a special for television."

I was not about to argue the point. What mattered here was our mutual desire to get the film made, whatever the medium. Indeed, his enthusiasm for the project was highly encouraging, going all the way to a promise to pay me $25,000 for the rights.

From this I gathered he had made his deal. NBC, Mobil Oil, Talent Associates, and *Eight Men Out*. Network, sponsor, producing organization, property.

"Well, I really hope it happens," I said, and promised I would do what I could to implement it.

As it turned out, there was little I could do. A fledgling New York moviemaker, Douglas Schmidt (a highly talented and successful stage designer), owned the option and had no intention of abandoning it. His writers had put in a year's work on their script and maintained high hopes of getting a Hollywood production.

Though I reported this to David, he was undeterred. He had producer Audrey Gellen go to work on it. Indeed, I met with their choice of writers, Edwin "Bud" Shrake, a scenarist and senior editor at *Sports Illustrated*, to discuss various possible approaches to the extremely complex story—a dry run, as it were, since no real work could begin until the rights became available. Though such a meeting seemed bizarre to me, I was riding the crest of Susskind's optimism. Sooner or later, I would get the rights back.

Meanwhile, there was my new work, *The Fox Is Crazy Too*, and though it was far from finished (I hadn't even shown it to my editor), Susskind wanted to see it.

"As soon as your editor has it, the big studios get their hands on it," he said.

"But I'm not sending it out to them."

"It doesn't matter. They see everything that's written." He explained that there are clerks at publishing houses and large literary agencies who are on studio payrolls, a whole network of spies and informers gathering hot new material, working furtively at the Xerox machines to sneak out copies. A spine-tingling notion, all right. Never had I felt so important as a writer.

Rough as the manuscript was, I showed it to him, and a week later he called.

"I want to buy *The Fox*," he said.

"You'll own all of me pretty soon," I quipped.

I would have predicted David would like the book, for it dealt with the folly of forensic psychiatry and the hypocrisy of the courts as seen through the eyes of an extremely talented rogue bent on beating the system.

As it turned out, he wanted to option *The Fox Is Crazy Too*, not to buy it. I agreed to that, but only on condition that I get the first crack at writing the screenplay. He objected. "You're a fine author, Eliot, not a screenwriter." I objected to *that*, having served my time in Hollywood and feeling perfectly competent in this field. Besides, I had seen what high-priced, multicredited screenwriters had done to other of my books—unshootable screenplays and a terrible movie such as *Breakout* (starring Charles Bronson), wherein three major screenwriters turned out a disastrous multimillion-dollar flop. With *The Fox*, I asked for $35,000 for my work, guaranteed. If he used my screenplay—and made the picture—I would get $40,000 more.

In the end, but only after I had created a structure for the scenario, he agreed. As for the option on the book itself, we settled on $5,000 as against an additional $95,000 if he went into production.

I was more than pleased, especially since I'd negotiated on my own, without benefit of an agent. I already had an attorney associated with the book (David Lubell, who represented Garrett Trapnell, the living protagonist of the story), and I immediately went to Lubell's office, requesting him to draw up a letter of agreement for Susskind's signature so that a contract might then be implemented as quickly as possible.

"But you need an agent!" people in the business insisted.

"Why? I know my needs better than any agent." I explained that I'd had top-level agents on earlier film projects, each of whom arranged deals that *excluded* me. ("It's the best we can do, Eliot," they'd say, "the producer simply insists on going with his own screenwriter"—who just happened to be the agent's client.)

"Maybe so," they persisted, "but you still need protection."

"From whom?"

"From Susskind, of course. He's a producer, isn't he?"

I laughed. Why would I need protection? Protection from what? What was Susskind going to do to me? We had made a deal. We'd even shaken hands on it. A lawyer would draw up whatever papers were necessary. What disasters could possibly happen that an agent could prevent? The thought of giving away 10 percent of my hard-earned income for such dubious representation bordered on the obscene.

"I'd trust David before I'd trust an agent," I said.

"You've been away from the business too long," I was warned.

In a way, I suppose that was true enough. I hadn't worked in television for eight or nine years, concentrating instead on writing books and magazine articles. And since I remained apart from all the usual hassling that accompanies a TV writer's life, no doubt there was a lot of scuttlebutt I hadn't heard.

Then I ran into a successful writer in a tennis locker room, an old friend whose judgment and values I'd always respected. I was not surprised that he'd heard of my new deals with Susskind. I was terribly surprised when he volunteered a solemn caveat.

"Be careful, El . . . "

"Oh, come off it."

He shook his head, amused at what he considered to be my blindness. "Are you all signed up?" he asked. "Contracts all executed? Has he paid you in full?"

"Well, no. Not yet."

"Have a good tennis game," he said ruefully.

I would learn, but slowly. Indeed, it might even be argued that the sordid events in this book would not have occurred if an agent had been handling these affairs. Certainly, agents will claim as much—just as psychiatrists will claim that the suicide victim would never have taken those pills had he or she remained in therapy. I reject such arguments as specious as well as statistically false, for there are at least as many writer-victims under the guidance of literary agents as there are suicides who are actively in therapy.

Still, lawyer or no lawyer, three months later there was still no signed agreement. One could only assume Susskind's motives for such dilatory tactics: since he knew he was the only producer involved, there was never any question of his losing the property.

When he finally had to confront Lubell and me, he actually retracted his offer of $5,000 for the option. He was very short of cash, he explained. Couldn't we reduce the figure to, say, $2,000? After all, he reassured us, he had every intention of making the film.

It was strange. Somehow he left me with the uneasy sense that it was *I* who was exploiting *him*. Hours later, I sat home replaying his pitch for sympathy, and I began to smolder over my easy gullibility.

"You look like you just slew a dragon," said my friend Janet. She liked to describe the way I was trying to look—always the opposite of the way I felt. Or so she thought. Actually, she was quite good at that game.

Janet was a lovely redheaded divorcée from Detroit, a professional singer trying to make a living on the stage. It was terribly frustrating to her that she had to make it as a waitress. She was bright and funny and, I thought, not nearly as tough as she pretended to be. I liked that.

She kicked off her shoes, rubbed her feet luxuriously against the rug to gratify an itch. She unbuttoned a sweated blouse, let it fall to the floor. She was en route to the shower, I knew, leaving a trail of clothes. Since she always picked them up, it didn't bother me. She would leave for work shortly, which did.

"How did it go?" I asked, knowing she'd been to see some agent about an audition.

"I was dynamite," she said.

"Sure, but what did *he* say?"

"Nothing. He wasn't there."

"Screwed again," I commented.

My concern for her plight in the midst of my own pleased me. I raised my glass of tinkling ice cubes as if in a toast.

"Better days."

She stopped in a doorway, stared back at me, taking a new feel of the scene. Since I was never much of a boozer, that alone had to catch her attention.

"What happened?" she asked.

I told her about the knocked-down option money, and we spent a few minutes beating Susskind around.

"Are you going to keep working on the script anyway?" she asked.

"Of course."

Since when did a writer wait for a signed contract before he began work?

In fact, I went to work eagerly, never doubting the validity of the agreement. Even the passage of time did not bother me. Susskind had told me to go to work. He had even called a few times to ask how it was going, eager for a look at the first act as soon as it was ready. Both Lubell and I kept asking about the contract, and he kept referring it to Ron Gilbert, his lieutenant who handled those details. Meanwhile, I trusted and worked. I really felt on the verge of a big breakthrough in my career. Great things were going to happen. My sparkling screenplay of *The Fox Is Crazy Too,* the coming publication of the book itself, the eventual filming of *Eight Men Out.*

Before the summer was over, I would sing a different tune.

3.

The trouble began with a letter dated June 24, 1975, signed by Michael Frankfurt, attorney for Douglas Schmidt. The key paragraph dumped the following complaint in my lap:

"This is to notify you that our client has been advised by Mr. David Susskind of Talent Associates, Ltd., that your contract with Mr. Schmidt violates a previous agreement entered into by you and Talent Associates, in that the rights that you have granted to our clients were heretofore granted to Talent Associates."

It was a stunner, all right. Apparently, Susskind had come up with that 1960 agreement between TA and me when I first went to work on the Black Sox story, in that case as "a researcher . . . to deliver to us in written form the product of your research work," a subsequent paragraph of which went on to claim that TA owned that research "perpetually and without encumbrance, all material you furnish hereunder."

(If that seemed unreasonably beneficial to TA, I may be excused my faulty negotiation. In those days, I didn't know any better: I had an agent to handle the deal.)

At this point, however, Susskind's reasoning was absolutely preposterous. To claim that the 1960 agreement tied up the rights to my book was akin to claiming ownership of the Empire State Building because you once took the architect to lunch. Susskind was saying, in effect, that I couldn't sell the rights to my own book!

I explained all this to Schmidt, emphasizing that the 1960 agreement had absolutely nothing to do with my book.

"It may be ludicrous to you, but my lawyer takes it very seriously."

I acknowledged that. Lawyers always take those things seriously.

Pressured by Ron Gilbert, Lawyer Frankfurt's next letter made no bones about his disquietude: "This letter is to request that you immediately obtain legal representation in order that we may communicate with someone who will understand the serious nature of the Talent Associates claim."

Beautiful. I could picture the resulting scenario. One $50-an-hour lawyer writing letters back and forth with another $50-an-hour lawyer, in a developing charade that would eventually lend dignity to Susskind's totally contemptible claim. As Frankfurt wrote: "I cannot understand how you are oblivious to the fact that you had entered into a prior contract with Talent Associates."

Again, beautiful. No doubt Susskind and Gilbert were enjoying this. After all, they were "creating a cloud over the title," presumably to intimidate Schmidt from pursuing the sale, thereby abetting their own chances of producing the film. That I was caught in the middle was totally irrelevant. Seeking advice, I spoke with one lawyer who informed me that I was actually liable to suit by both parties!

I advised Susskind that I did not appreciate these tactics; he was turning what had first seemed like a joke into an instrument of trouble. It wasn't fair to Schmidt or to me. He had no right to do that. Whatever his lawyers might make of it, his claim of prior rights was ludicrous and he knew it as well as I did. His response was that I need not be concerned. Since Schmidt (by my own claim) had no chance to sell his script anyway, might not a little pressure such as this force a compromise?

"I'm going to make this picture!" he kept telling me.

4.

By mid-August there was still no signed agreement with Talent Associates for *The Fox Is Crazy Too.* I did what writers are supposed to do: I hollered at my lawyer, David Lubell. Why hadn't he consummated the agreement? Where was the $2,000 for the option on the book? And the $11,666.66 (first payment on the $35,000) for the screenplay?

"It takes two to make a deal," he wailed. "I can't pin him down. He keeps changing the numbers. He takes from here, then switches what he gives you there."

Which, I suppose, is precisely why writers have lawyers.

Inevitably, those warnings about Susskind's tactics began to fester—enough to feed any writer's paranoia about how and when and even *if* he is going to be paid.

After all, this was the Jungle.

Then David had his producer Diana Kerew call.

"We're all waiting for your screenplay of *The Fox*, Eliot . . ."

"And I'm waiting for a contract and a check, Diana."

"Oh . . . "

Several more weeks elapsed during which I continued working. I was, in fact, approaching the end of what I felt to be a rough but sturdy first draft—an indication of how long it had been since we had allegedly made the deal.

Then, finally, a check arrived.

Not $11,666.66, the first third of $35,000, but $10,000. Substantial, yes, but why not the full sum we'd agreed on?

I stared at the check in bewilderment. Should I send it back, advising them of the error? What sort of nonsense was this! Does Talent Associates pay only part of their rent? Their phone bill? Does Susskind get a cut rate at "21"?

Said Ron Gilbert: "Look, Eliot, ten thousand is a lot of money. Take it. We'll straighten it all out on signing."

Ten thousand dollars is a lot of money, so I banked it.

Then, compliantly, I delivered the first third of the screenplay.

Life in the Jungle would then become even more treacherous.

"It doesn't work, Eliot," Diana reported a week later. "We don't like it at all."

"Well, let's sit down and go over it," I said. I respected Diana as an editor. She had been a big help with the first manuscript of the book itself, offering valuable suggestions for cutting. Indeed, it was always important that I get this sort of editorial assistance, having long since learned that weaknesses in first drafts were more readily detected by others. In all my work, whatever the medium, I rely on writer friends to fill this need.

I was, then, severely jolted at her response:

"There's really no point in it . . ." she said. "We all love you here. You know that. But we don't think you can write a screenplay. A lot of fine authors can't. It's a very special talent, you know."

I didn't know how to respond. It just didn't make any sense to me. That there was nothing salvageable about my script seemed too crushing to cope with.

I withdrew as gracefully as I could, leaving the future of the project up in the air until I could come to terms with this rejection.

It really chopped my feet out from under me. When I opened the screenplay again, I shuddered. Was it really that worthless?

Since I wrote it, how could I possibly know?

It was like asking a starving cat to guard the milk, as they say.

Better that I ask a well-fed dairyman.

I went at the problem with gusto and trembling, making six copies of the unfinished scenario, then delivering it to six successful screenwriters I knew, talented multicredited professionals such as Oscar-winner Ring Lardner, Jr. (*M°A°S°H°*), and Oscar-nominee Walter Bernstein (*The Front*).

"Tell me what you think," I said, giving them no details of my plight. "It is good? Bad? How good? How bad? Be as critical as possible."

They agreed.

For the next day or so I was like a convict on death row sweating out the governor's pardon.

"Let's go to the movies," Janet offered.

"I hate movies," I said.

"Maybe we could see a real stinker and you could tell me how bad the screenplay is."

"Very funny." I shuddered.

But she wasn't about to quit. "Hey look, they're playing *Alice*

Doesn't Live Here Anymore," she said. "I'd *love* to see that again."

Alice, of course, was an extremely well-received film produced by David Susskind himself.

"Janet doesn't live here anymore," I said.

"Sore loser," she mumbled.

Then the phone started ringing, and suddenly everything was roses.

To a man, those who read my scenario thought highly of it. There was a reassuring agreement about its strengths and weaknesses, but especially the former. They found the central character fascinating and were caught up by the suspense involved in his fate. And when I pressed them, they laughed at any question as to my ability to write it.

If this proved a salve to my ego, it did not alter my status with Talent Associates. The rejection had been so summary, one had to speculate on the real motives behind it. The key, as I saw it, was Susskind's failure to execute the agreement. He simply abandoned the entire project. In fact, he had played possum with the whole matter from the start, neither committing to it nor rejecting. Was it because he had overextended himself by initiating too many projects and had to pull back? Had he not actually pleaded for a reduction of the $5,000 option fee on these same grounds, then refused to pay even that?

If there were any doubts about his disenchantment, they were dispelled quickly enough. The matter of payment remained, signed contract or no. Though I was not to do any further work on the script, I was owed the balance of that agreed-upon $35,000, for payment had not been conditional.

One more conversation with Diana Kerew, however, laid bare what was in store for me.

"David is fully aware that he made an agreement with you," she said. "And he will, somehow, go through with it if you insist on it. But really, Eliot . . ."

It was a wonderment, all right. Words blurred into a meaningless babble. I was actually being asked if I wanted to be paid!

It hit me like a sharp jab to the button of my jaw. Something was wrong, something I did not know about. Nothing read the way it sounded, nothing appeared as it met the eye.

What they really seemed to be saying was: You aren't going to demand this money, are you, because we sure as hell have no intention of giving it to you.

Which meant, of course, that I'd have to go to war merely trying to get it.

Out of the Jungle, into the Quicksand.

"Why don't you simply tell him you want the money, just to see what happens," Janet suggested. "I mean, what do you have to lose?"

I considered that. Further, I considered putting up a fight for it, even hiring a special lawyer. Then I speculated on the cost of winning in time and money and, presumably, compromise. To deal with Susskind was to know the art of compromise. Carried to extreme, you had to compromise the compromise, eventually compromising the deal until you owed *him* money. I could even picture my lawyer ending up in agreement. ("After all, Eliot, you didn't actually finish the script!") But above all, even if I finally managed to receive payment, wouldn't Susskind force me to abandon all rights to the screenplay in exchange?

It was marvelous, the way an embattled mind could unravel the hairiest snarls. What seemed like the most self-destructive solution suddenly emerged as quite the opposite—and vice versa.

I went with my instincts—and skirted the Quicksand.

I wanted out. Completely out. The romance had turned sour. The chemistry was stirring up angry bubbles in the test tubes. It would be far better to have nothing more to do with Susskind. All deals were off. I would retreat with my two books intact, put *The Fox Is Crazy Too* (which would be published in a few months) back on the movie market, and when the option on *Eight Men Out* expired in May, I would try to sell it elsewhere. Let Susskind keep his money and whatever he chose to make of his chickenshit victory. I would take my losses and break clean.

"You're out of your head," Janet said, but not with any real conviction.

"Diana," I said on the phone, totally without rancor, "tell David to forget it. I don't want his money."

There was silence at those words. I could only guess she was thunderstruck. I wondered, too, if Susskind was listening on an extension.

"Good-bye to you all," I said, and hung up.

"Terrific!" Janet chided me. "You must represent me when I get a job."

I took the rest of the day off.

5.

The truth was, I really felt good about it. Though I couldn't explain why, I knew it was a victory for me—even though I became the local joke.

"Another victory like that and you'll be bankrupt."

Or, "On those terms, you'll have every producer in town calling you."

Or, "By the way, how much are you paying your publisher as an advance on your next book?"

I could even hear a thousand literary agents laughing at me.

I didn't care. Some people have to pay for their liberation, but that didn't make it any less satisfying.

I could even describe myself as serenely defiant, a condition that bordered on Nirvana itself.

Witness, for example, a significant reflection of what I had become:

I am second on line at a supermarket check-out counter when a well-dressed elderly lady muscles her way in, pushing a loaded cart obliquely in front of mine.

"Lady, please . . . There's a line here," I say, but she stares straight ahead, body rigid, pretending not to hear. Her eyes are fastened on the bodies in front of her, the forward wheels of her cart pressuring mine.

She is so much the bully, I have to laugh.

"Lady, you really shouldn't do that," I persist.

But there is no compromise in her stance. In fact, at the first sign of movement at the counter, she rams her cart in front of mine.

I know, I know. It's a trivial matter. I'm not even in a hurry. In one form or another, we've all seen this sort of thing happen. The archetypical enemy of the people, the insidious agent of our disharmony, the provocateur of our paranoia. It is as if the madness of the way we live is suddenly capsulized by this act, and circumstance has appointed me its arbiter.

But what can I do? In that instant, I don't know, only that I must do something, for have I not been chosen to protect the integrity of this line, of the countless lines in every supermarket in America?

Inspired, I rise to the occasion. Without another word I lift a large paper sack from her cart, and send a dozen oranges rolling over the floor. Then, several cans of applesauce, a loaf of bread, a roll of kitchen towels. Immediately, she comes alive, screaming above the clatter in a fierce Germanic accent. "Vhat are you doing! Stop him! Stop him!" This time, I am the silent one, methodically emptying her cart: aluminum foil, two cans of tuna fish, a paper carton of tea bags. Behind me, someone is laughing. A young male voice calls out "All riiiiight!" It is really quite beautiful. And finally, to a sustained burst of applause that would have moved even a talent such as Baryshnikov, I arrive at the cashier myself.

For weeks afterward, people would smile and wave at me in that market. Others, like the dry cleaner, the barber, the newspaperman, regarded me with new respect.

One simply could not put a price tag on such a victory.

Thus, the fall of 1975 segued into the winter of 1976.

Then, in February, a call from a friend in Hollywood contained the following dialogue:

"I see that Susskind is finally doing your book."

"What?" I asked. "What book?"

"*Eight Men Out,*" he said, then read me the bad news: " 'Talent Associates, in production on "Say it Ain't So, Joe." ' "

The title was a dead giveaway, the famous quote of a young boy confronting the great "Shoeless" Joe Jackson after he had confessed to throwing the World Series.

"Yeah, big announcement in *Variety,*" he went on.

"But he can't do that!" I exploded, the desperate man trying to convince himself.

"Why not?"

"Well, for one thing, he doesn't own the rights."

"Heh, heh. Famous last words."

Immediately, my throat locked as though I'd been marooned in the Sahara Desert. There was no way I could have continued the conversation. I rasped a feeble good-bye, then rushed to the water faucet. And when I'd put out the fire, I rushed to the phone to confront the arsonist.

He was, of course, in hiding.

"Sorry, Eliot, David is busy in a meeting," said his secretary.

He did not call back that afternoon. Or the following day. I tried again, and again he was too busy to speak to me. On the day after, she said he was out of the office.

I finally got the message: he did not want to talk to me.

"Ha ha," Janet said, "now you know what it's like to be a waitress trying to be a singer."

"If I could sing, I wouldn't be a writer," I replied.

Then we had a quick reprise on old speculations as to what she would do if Susskind chanced to eat lunch where she worked.

"Hot soup in the lap," she said. "It's a killer."

"No," I countered, "you've got to work on him slowly. First, a pat of butter on his lapel. Then, maybe a drink spilled on his sleeve . . . You've got to *build* to the big one."

She shook her head in simulated awe. "You writers . . ."

I put in a call to Susskind's associate, Ron Gilbert. For another two days, he, too, was unreachable.

Still, I did not abandon the possibility that the announcement was merely a statement of prospects. This was February. The option on *Eight Men Out* expired in May. Susskind, like other producers, made long-term projections. It could be that the announcement in *Variety* was merely his way of declaring his intent, to stake out his claim, as it were, presumably to scare off any competition.

Then why didn't he or Ron Gilbert return my phone calls?

"I can't imagine," Janet teased me.

"If I ever got to be an executive, I'd return *every* phone call immediately. And I'd be completely candid. I mean, I'd say, 'Eliot, we're screwing you. Tough shit, but you know how it is in the Jungle.' That sort of thing. I'd win your respect. Right?"

"Right."

"Then we could trust each other. We could always work together on another project."

"Right."

"Christ, what madness!"

"Right."

Unable to contain my anxieties, I called Diana Kerew at home, not wishing to put her to any embarrassment at work.

"Yes, it's true, Eliot," she explained. "It's really no secret. We have a script written by Sidney Carroll, all taken from his own research."

"——!"

"Well, you know how hard we tried to get the rights to your book," she went on. "We simply had to go to the public domain. I'm sorry, but what else could we do?"

Everything stuck in my throat. Nor was there any point in pursuing this with her. Diana was merely a hireling. I thanked her for telling me the bad news and spared her my rage, then spent a horrible night with it.

It was all so depressing, I could hardly make sense of it. Yet it was simple enough. The Black Sox Scandal was history, and no author could own any part of history. My problem was that I could not believe Susskind would do such a thing. I could not believe *anyone* would do such a thing. But Susskind was doing it. He was going to make a film for television about the Black Sox Scandal, and that would be it. Because of its special nature, all others who sought to deal with this material were dead, myself included. *Eight Men Out* would immediately become a dead property.

Once again, I tried to reach Susskind, but to no avail. This time,

I got Ron Gilbert, if only to deliver the message. If I were to be butchered in this affair, at least I would go down screaming at someone.

"You devious bastards!" I went at him: "Tell Susskind I think he's a Grade A sonovabitch!" And so on, the sort of adolescent vituperation that New York taxi drivers use on slow-moving drivers of Connecticut station wagons. I must have bellowed for a minute or two, then hung up, feeling twice as ridiculous afterward.

Infinitely worse than ridiculous, of course. I was engulfed by the kind of rage that derives only from helplessness. Facing a situation riddled as it was with such idiotic components, I could be excused, perhaps, for acting in kind—which is another way of saying that I went to see a lawyer.

"There's nothing you can do," I was advised, "unless Susskind has taken the actual structure of your book, or unless you can prove he has used material that is in your book only, he has a perfect right to go ahead with what he can learn from the public domain."

"But what if my book is considered to be the definitive work," I argued. "What if I brought you a list of the most distinguished people in the sporting world, in publishing, in the media, even, and all of them tied the Black Sox Scandal with my book. What then? Doesn't *that* mean anything?"

"Only to you, El . . ."

"Then why do movie companies always buy rights to books? Why did Susskind try in the first place?"

"Mostly to make things simple, to avoid trouble, to dignify the project. If the book is available, why not buy it?"

"Dammit, there's got to be a way to stop him!"

"Take my advice: forget it."

The trouble with lawyers is their extremely limited options: they will either sue, write a letter, or tell you to forget it.

How could I forget it? This was my book. It wasn't just money. It was the product of two years' work, plus all the years that had preceded them. Could you say that to a man who has just been cuckolded?

Which left me dangling, as usual.

"Suck and the world sucks with you," said Janet. "Dangle and you dangle alone."

"Well, there's got to be *something* I can do!" I said, a feeble ejaculation if there ever was one, and the room fell into dead silence for a while. It was weird, for the next words spoken seemed to take on an exaggerated significance as a result.

"What you need is a Godfather," she said.

It was incredible, the way that ludicrous thought suddenly raced through me as a genuine panacea, as effective as a wet sponge across a blackboard. I conjured up glittering images of two large men in tight overcoats moving into Susskind's office, all very polite, of course, making slick unrefusable offers in my behalf.

"Say it ain't so, David Susskind."

Right?

A man could get transported to the Garden of Eden with such idyllically convenient configurations. What jolted me at the moment was the fantastic thought that it was *all based on reality,* for I'd actually had the chance for a Godfather of the first water. Not some small-time Mafiosi, but the mightiest of the mighty. I'd had him, solidly, right in the palm of my hand.

And what seemed so fascinating, at the moment, was that it was directly related to *Eight Men Out.*

The nexus was a bookmaker named Jeremiah Kelly, a highly regarded member of his trade, who listed among his clients some of the most prestigious business and professional men in the East. To any New York betting man in the fifties and sixties, Jerry Kelly was a name that meant as much as Vladimir Horowitz meant to a piano player.

One fine autumn morning in 1963, this man walked into the offices of Holt, Rinehart and Winston, peeled off $1,800 cash, and walked out with 500 copies of *Eight Men Out.* These he sent out as gifts to his distinguished clients. "A must read!" he described it.

It was the sort of thing that should happen to all writers.

"You really ought to give him a call," my editor, Howard Cady, had suggested.

Jerry was delighted that I did, and I joined him at lunch at his daily hangout, Dinty Moore's on Forty-sixth Street, where he had his own table a few feet from the reservation phone. As we ate, the phone would ring, sometimes for reservations, but mostly for Jerry. He would lean over, listen, then respond with a simple "Yeah." That was all he ever said. He never wrote anything down, but tucked the bet into his remarkable memory, then returned to our conversation. He told me about all the people who had read my book and had personally thanked him: corporation presidents, union leaders, judges, theatrical producers, bankers. He said he had never come across a book like mine before and that he was an avid reader.

Then, a few weeks later, he invited some of his choice clients to lunch with me as guest of honor, and I sat in the midst of more power than a meeting of the President's cabinet. People like the president of General Dynamics, chairman of the board of a Rockefeller foundation, public relations director of the Teamsters Union. I ate corned beef and cabbage and listened to enough compliments of my work to choke a glutton.

I was sipping coffee when I felt a polite hand on my shoulder and looked up to a dark-haired man in a gray suit and a very bright blue necktie.

"Mr. Asinof," he said quietly, "the Big Man would like to see you."

The Big Man? I looked at Jerry Kelly, who smiled and nodded, then leaned over to whisper the magic name:

"Frank Costello."

I did not gag, nor did the coffee cup quiver in my hand. I doubt if I even paled as I calmly returned the cup to the saucer, vaguely aware that to cover myself I was pretending that this was all a joke. The truth was, I was frightened. The name alone was enough to intimidate me. The way I saw it, Costello was going to nail me to the wall for defaming gamblers, particularly Arnold Rothstein. I pictured Abe Attell, furious at my interpretation of his slimy ways (one reviewer had written that "Attell weaves through Asinof's book like a deadly spider"), telling Costello that I was a dirty rat. But it was the material about Rothstein that worried me most, for Rothstein had been Costello's mentor and friend.

It was not that way, as it turned out. Quite the contrary, the voice above the bright blue tie went on: "The Big Man says to tell you, you wrote a right book."

"Well, thanks," I said, taking his words to mean it was not a "wrong" one. "I mean, tell him thanks a lot. I'm really glad he liked it."

Sure. Even Abe Attell later told me how much he liked it.

"He wants to see you, Mr. Asinof. This afternoon, okay?"

Jerry was smiling like a proud father, nodding his head at me. Obviously, this was not without his knowledge. As for me, I remained in fear, though no longer certain as to what I should be frightened about. I needed time to adjust. I was not one to look a gift horse in the mouth (or was I?), but then, was it really a gift?

"This afternoon?" I felt myself squirming. "Oh, I can't . . ." as though suddenly remembering. "I'm sorry. I can't make it this afternoon."

Blue Tie took it kindly enough. "We'll call you, then," he said. The hand patted my shoulder once, then left.

After lunch I casually asked Jerry what he thought the Big Man wanted. Kelly shrugged. "What he wants, he gets," he said, a non-answer that added heavy layers to my question.

I slept on it, as they say—or, more accurately, spent the night *not* sleeping on it, bothered as I was by the implication of dark, sinister forces that might either betray me or most certainly corrupt me. "At least, go see him!" a friend urged. "What in hell do you have to lose!" What, indeed. I pictured that scene, seated across from him in my best suit and tie while he smiled in his smooth, compelling manner (with Blue Tie standing close by), delivering the word in that famous throaty voice while I strained to hear: "You're a fine writer, Eliot. I envy the talent of a fine writer." Then he'd say that he was getting old and thought maybe he'd like to set the record straight. "I don't want to die with people thinking I did terrible things," he'd say. "I did a lot of good things, and that's what they should remember about me." I'd be nodding my head, a glass of his best Scotch in one hand, an Upmann smoking in the other, wondering how I could refuse the honor of being his biographer. What possible reason could I have for refusing? "Why refuse at all?" my friends asked. Why? Because I knew that if I were Mr. Costello's writer I'd be writing what he wanted me to write. I'd be delivering the message the way Blue Tie delivered the message. Could anyone imagine a writer turning out a manuscript that Mr. Costello found *un*complimentary? In some ingenious way, wasn't that why Mr. Costello was seeking me out: precisely because I'd written critically of Arnold Rothstein et al., wouldn't that bring credibility to my biography of him?

I was overreacting, of course. After all, Mr. Costello was known to be a gentleman. He lived at the respectable Century Apartments on Central Park West, barely six blocks from me. He got along with his neighbors, entertained his friends, tipped the doormen for getting him taxis. He didn't even carry a gun, I was told. It was childish of me to think I'd be dropped into the East River with my feet in concrete.

Then, early the following morning, he called. Or Blue Tie did, and finally, there was the famous throaty voice slashing in my ear.

"I gotta tell you, your book about the Black Sox and all, it was wonderful."

"Thank you, Mr. Costello."

"The way you caught the whole feel of the thing, that was something, all right. Especially Arnold Rothstein."

Well, that was a relief.

"Thanks, I appreciate the compliment."

"I'd like to talk to you, Eliot . . ."

Eliot, he called me. Like an old friend, by God.

Somehow, I had to know it all, right then and there. I wanted to hear him say what he wanted of me. It seemed terribly important that he say the words.

"What about?" I dared to ask.

"I've got a few ideas, you know. I'd like to talk to a writer like you. There comes a time when a man thinks about maybe putting them down."

Well, there it was. The door was being opened for me. All I had to do was walk in and, after a chat, I'd walk out rich. It didn't take a meeting with some superagent to know how much any publisher would pay for Costello's memoirs.

I took a deep breath and covered the phone to muffle a quick clearing of my throat. But when I spoke again—"Well, that really interests me, Mr. Costello"—my voice was an octave lower, its tones almost unrecognizable to my own ear, and I was horrified that he might think I was mimicking him. Quickly, I coughed into the phone, apologizing politely, then finally managed a reasonably normal tone: ". . . but I'm up to my neck in a new book right now, I mean, I really don't see how I could do it justice."

That's what I told him. I'd rejected Frank Costello. I hadn't really planned it, it just came out that way.

"Well . . ." he said slowly, his disappointment obvious, "then all I can do is wish you the best of luck," and he sounded so sincere, for an instant I considered the possibility of reversing myself.

I thanked him and hung up, enormously relieved that it was all over—until I began to wonder if I had misread the scenario. Could one reject the Godfather? ("What Costello wants, he gets," Jerry Kelly had said.) I began to picture him growing increasingly annoyed, planning ways to get to me. After all, what was one struggling writer to a man who had bought out Tammany Hall and controlled the politics of New York City itself?

I heard nothing for several months. Then, late one June morning in 1964, the phone rang, and it was Jerry.

"Long time, no see," he said, then invited me to join him for lunch.

"I'll try to make it," I said.

"Not good enough," he went on. "Be here no later than twelve-fifteen."

I took his persistence to be nothing more than politeness, and told him I'd be there. As it turned out, however, my work was going well, and time rushed by; when I looked up from my typewriter, it was well after one. I called Moore's to apologize, but the line was busy. Twice. I made my own lunch and forgot about it.

That night, the lead story on the news, and the next morning's headlines, related to the arrest of Frank Costello and his luncheon partner, the bookmaker Jeremiah Kelly, at Dinty Moore's. The charge was vagrancy, though Kelly had $7,400 in $100 bills, and

Costello had $6. As *The New York Times* reported the incident, a federal agent approached the Kelly table and, recognizing Frank Costello, asked:

"What are you doing?"

"I'm eating, that's all."

"What are your means of support?"

"I'm retired."

Actually, the Feds wanted Kelly for an alleged failure to purchase a $50 wagering-tax stamp. Both were taken to the police station and booked. Kelly, it seemed, ended up in the Federal House of Detention for the night. Costello was immediately released. The irony of the scene was heightened by the presence of U.S. Attorney Robert Morgenthau, who happened to be lunching with them. Morgenthau was said to describe Kelly as "a society bookie who handles five hundred thousand dollars a year in bets."

There, but for the grace of my typewriter, went I.

"And that," I said to Janet, "was my big chance for a proper Godfather."

"Damn, you'd have been *untouchable*. Nobody would dare sue you for anything," she sighed. "You'd be above the law itself!"

"Except for vagrancy, of course."

"I'd make one helluva moll," she mused.

6.

Unable to reach either Susskind or Costello, I was left to seethe in frustration.

"Take my advice, forget it," the lawyer had said.

As for me, the thought of losing that book so rankled, I even began losing sleep over it. There had to be *something* I could do, some move I could make, at least to *try* to stop him.

The best I could come up with was a feeble notion to call NBC, not knowing what I would say or to whom. Indeed, I could picture the telephonic runaround in store for me: from switchboard to secretary of an out-of-the-office executive and back to the switchboard for a double play.

Then out of the blue, I remembered Carl Lindeman, vice-president of "NBC Sports," an acquaintance from way back during his producing days.

"Give me Carl Lindeman, please," I said.

And a moment later, his friendly voice: "Hey, Eliot, how are you?"

"Fine, fine. Say, Carl, would you happen to know who might be in charge of a project relating to my book on the Black Sox?"

"*Eight Men Out?*" He was right there, all right. "It's Bill Storke . . ." and in three quick shakes of the lamb's tail, he had me connected.

"Hello, Eliot," Storke said with such surprising warmth I wondered if I knew him too. It was almost as though he'd been expecting my call.

Did he know anything about the Black Sox Scandal project with Talent Associates? He replied that he did, intimately so. In fact, the whole project had been initiated in his office!

I took the bull by the horns and told him my tale of woe, blow by blow, right from the beginning. The thrust of my report was simple enough: Susskind had wanted to buy the rights, but since I did not own them to sell, he had apparently gone ahead without them.

I had no notion of what to expect in response, perhaps nothing more than a polite and sympathetic hearing.

For a moment, Storke said nothing. "Executive silence" they call it.

Then he stunned me.

"This is absolutely appalling! Are you telling me this has all taken place without your involvement? I've assumed that you've been employed as a consultant."

"Consultant? Well, I *did* meet with Bud Shrake last spring . . ."

"Shrake? What about Sidney Carroll? Haven't you been working with him?"

"I've never met him."

"And you haven't received any money for this, Eliot?"

"No."

"You were supposed to get ten thousand dollars for the rights to your book!"

I wondered: Was *that* the source of the $10,000 Susskind paid me for a totally different project?

"But I don't own the rights," I told Storke. "How can I take any money if I don't own the rights?"

Another pause, this time to regroup his thoughts.

"Eliot, this is terrible. Absolutely terrible. A year ago, David came in here with your book. We all knew how wonderful it was. He said he wanted to make a television film about it, a dramatization based on your book, hopefully to get it on for World Series time. As I recall, Herb Schmerz at Mobil was interested. The project was approved and I had a check sent to Talent Associates to get it rolling. I was told that you were involved from the beginning!" Again a pause. I could hear his throat clearing with indignation. "Eliot, you know, you could slap a nasty lawsuit on NBC, and Talent Associates, for this . . ."

"I have no intention of suing anyone, Bill," I replied. "I'm not the litigious type."

"Well, I'm glad of that. And I'm glad you told me about this," he went on. "The important thing to me, as I'm sure it is for everyone, is to have the best possible script. That certainly means working with you. There's no question but that you are the expert in this matter and we would insist that you become involved. I'm going to call David and get this straightened out."

I hung up the phone and let out a shriek of joy. Home run with the bases loaded. I began to dance, sort of a cross between Hitler's famous little jig after conquering France and an NFL touchdown dance by a black receiver who has just caught one in the end zone.

"The tide has turned!" I cried out.

"Take the rest of the day off," Janet said.

It was only the beginning. Less than an hour later, Susskind finally called. He was very friendly and relaxed about the whole thing, almost as if there were really no problems at all.

"You have nothing to worry about, Eliot," he said. "We made a deal, you and I. Even if we can't use your book, I'm going through with our deal. What was it, twenty-five thousand? I'm going to get the Black Sox Scandal on the air," he repeated. "And you and I know that nobody else can do it."

I told him I wanted to see the script. I wanted to know exactly what was going on. He replied that Sidney Carroll was one of the finest writers in the East and that he'd done a remarkable job in spite of the limitations. "I'm sure you'll appreciate that . . ."

He didn't send the script to me. And when I called a few days later, again he became unavailable. It then occurred to me to contact Sidney Carroll himself. He was a colleague. Wouldn't a fellow writer best understand the problems of another? Certainly, *he* would show me the script.

When I reached him on the phone, he was warm and gracious.

"Can we meet, Sidney? I'd like to talk to you."

We made a luncheon date a few days ahead, but he was unable to keep it. He would call me in a day or two to make another date. He didn't. I called him, leaving a message with his answering service. He returned the call a day later, apologizing that he'd been busy, could we make it the following week? I said okay, if that was his earliest free time. He promised to call on Monday.

He didn't, and I heard nothing all that week as well.

"How does that victory dance go again?" asked Janet.

On Friday, I called Bill Storke again.

He seemed very surprised.

"I thought everything had been worked out," he said. "David told me that you and he had agreed, that you've been working with them."

It was so far from the truth, I was embarrassed. Here was a

network executive doing business with a leading television production company, and, to put it mildly, serious misconceptions were dominating the dialogues.

"Nothing has been accomplished, Bill. Absolutely nothing." I told him that I couldn't reach David, and that Sidney, too, seemed to have been ducking me. "I still haven't even seen the script."

"What!" He was genuinely shocked at that. "I'll get a script to you immediately." I could hear him telling his secretary to get a messenger. "I want to know what you think of it, Eliot. I'm leaving for Los Angeles this afternoon. I'll be there all weekend. Call me at the Bel Air Hotel, collect. Will you?"

I said I would. Hardly an hour later, the script arrived, and soon enough, both Sidney and David called, Sidney to make a date with me, finally, and David to be reassuring. I told David I was going to read the script and Sidney that I would call *him* back.

Incredibly, an hour later, another hand-delivered document arrived, this one from Talent Associates. It was a letter of agreement dated April 1, 1976 (the preceding day), wherein I would be paid $25,000, the significant paragraph reading as follows: "You hereby sell, license, assign and grant to us all rights of every kind and nature (except publication) in and to the Book *(Eight Men Out)* in any and all media, throughout the Universe, in perpetuity."

It was wild. A week ago, I couldn't even get them on the phone. Now, I was being offered $25,000 for the book rights I did not own, by the very organization that claimed to have owned them in perpetuity.

Finally, then, I sat down to read the script.

Admittedly, one could seriously question my capacity to judge it. It is hardly the better part of wisdom to put a victim on the jury at the trial of a thief. No one could possibly come to a reading with a greater overlay of disenchantment than I.

On the other hand, there was that $25,000 payoff agreement to mitigate my prejudices, its official arrival so artfully timed, it could take a man's breath away. The way I saw it, the more I liked the script, the closer I would be to banking the money.

Indeed, I had to laugh at the temptation, remembering an incident while working at Columbia Pictures in Hollywood when a screenwriter named Guy Trosper gleefully dropped in at my office with a paperback Western in hand.

"What's the book?" I asked.

"Harry Cohn just handed it to me. 'Read it, let me know what you think,' he said."

Trosper laughed as he riffled through the pages in a few seconds. He would pick up $2,500 a week as screenwriter if he liked the book and nothing if he didn't.

"I like it," he said at once. "Good plot, lots of solid action. Make a damn good picture, you know?"

Sure.

I would have liked that kind of simplicity with "Say It Ain't So, Joe."

So, at last, I read it—straight through, wham bam, almost as rapidly as my fingers could flip the pages.

What I read was a glimpse of hell itself, for the script had the story all wrong. Not merely with inaccuracies, but outright distortions. I was thoroughly aware of the need for taking dramatic license with facts, but how could anyone justify the tainting of an innocent victim of the scandal (Buck Weaver) with actual complicity! Or the conception of the World Series fix itself by the wrong parties! Or the distortion of the cover-up that began even before the Series had ended, a cover-up that got at the very causes of the fix as well as its outcome! Instead, the scenario was terribly off-balance, overloaded by a repetitive game-by-game account of the manipulations of the gamblers, as if such petty details carried special significance. They didn't. What's more, they were inaccurate. They didn't happen, they couldn't have happened; even the premises were wrong.

After two readings, I was terribly depressed. The entire scandal had been trivialized, its participants turned into caricatures, its incredibly dramatic happenings untouched. It read as though someone had repeated a small part of a big story heard from thirdhand sources and the writer had taken off on it.

I went to the fridge for a beer. I took a few cool swallows, then reread the script, finishing the beer and the script together. I closed the covers and speculated on its failings. After all, they didn't have the rights to my book as a source. No doubt Susskind had warned Sidney about that, to keep clear of the specifics of *Eight Men Out* and hold to what he could find in old newspaper reports. It was like describing a dinner after merely reading the menu.

With an eye on what I might say to Bill Storke, I gave the script still another reading, marking those scenes with the most-jarring distortions. There were so many items, major and minor, that dug at my sensitivities, I put the script aside, aware that I had best reappraise the work after a cooling-off period. Then there was that little matter of $25,000 I could have for the asking and I was not going to help anyone by beating it down with a baseball bat.

When I picked it up again the following day, my approach had changed to one of constructive interest. After all, Storke was soliciting my help as an advisor. If there was a way to make the story work, I would be the one to supply it.

He was immediately available when I called and, I felt, extremely eager to hear what I had to say. I told him that the script "showed serious inaccuracies, unavoidable under the circumstances, but terribly jarring." He immediately asked if they could be corrected, and I assured him they could. Relieved, he then said he would arrange a meeting upon his return wherein all the participants would be assembled and the problems ironed out.

Perfect, I thought. Absolutely perfect. I would set up the revisions, the script would be accurate, the option with Doug Schmidt would run out, and I would collect the cherished $25,000.

"I don't like it," Janet said.

"What's not to like?"

"You be careful. They'll iron *you* out."

"Nonsense. I'm holding very good cards."

"Hoo hah," she said.

At ten in the morning, April 8, the big meeting was held in Storke's office at NBC. Present were Storke, of course; Fred Brogger, Susskind's partner at TA (whom I had never met); Diana Kerew, line producer; Delbert Mann, a seasoned director of films and television dramas, assigned to this project; a lawyer from NBC whose name I didn't catch; and myself.

Storke, whom I also met for the first time, was a distinguished and good-looking executive in middle years, well-tailored, well-spoken, with a pleasant friendly manner that belied the frantic nature of his occupation. The office was a large, bright corner room on the executive fourth floor of the RCA Building, replete with a spacious davenport, coffee table, and club chairs. We were an uncrowded, smiling half-dozen professionals, sipping coffee from Styrofoam cups, all very friendly of course.

Then Storke began by reviewing what had brought us all together.

"It seems we have a serious problem," he began, his tones appropriately ominous, I was pleased to note. "I'm sorry David is not here because there is a lot he has to account for." Fine, I thought; there was no question as to where he stood. "A year ago, David came to me with Eliot's book *Eight Men Out*. 'Read it,' he said. 'Herb Schmerz is interested. I think it would make a fine show.' I read it, as did others, and we all agreed. As a result, NBC sent thirty thousand dollars to Talent Associates to secure the rights to the book and get the project moving. Eventually, Sidney Carroll was hired to write it, with our approval. The script was finished. We liked it. It turned out that IBM [replacing Mobil Oil as sponsor] liked it with reservations. But all along, I thought that Eliot was involved as a technical advisor, lending his expertise. Then I heard that this was not the case, this was not the case at all. Talent Associates has *never* secured the rights, Eliot has *not* been involved, the book we allegedly bought has never been bought at all!"

41

His indignation was absolutely marvelous, and I bit my lip to contain any unseemly show of pleasure. The way I felt, I would have given half my equity in the project to have had Susskind present.

"Now, suppose you explain this," he said, directing himself to Fred Brogger.

Brogger, who was well prepared, leaped at the offer. "What you say is true enough, Bill. We tried to secure the rights but were unable to. We tried for a year. Eliot told us he thought he could get them back, but it turned out that he couldn't. So we simply went to the public domain. Now let's be clear about this, Bill. Sidney Carroll and his son, David, did a lot of very valuable research. David went to Chicago and dug into the records. He read everything that was available. It must be stated here that there is still a big mystery surrounding what happened in the Black Sox Scandal. Without meaning any disrespect for Eliot's book, it doesn't supply all the answers . . ."

At this point, as though on cue, Diana Kerew interceded: "Eliot himself admitted that, Bill. He told us he had to fictionalize. Why, he even invented characters!"

How artful that was! Diana was referring to two made-up names in the book, conceived on advice of an attorney, the sole purpose being to protect myself against plagiarism. Two fictitious characters were inserted that existed nowhere but from my typewriter, designed to prevent screenwriters from stealing the story and claiming their material was from the public domain. Now it was being used against me, and in precisely the sort of situation I had set out to thwart! Diana had taken that wonderful moment when I'd warned Susskind about them, refusing to identify them through all his repeated probing, and now used it to belittle my book!

Nonetheless, I said nothing. I felt secure on that davenport with Storke on the attack. I was holding the big cards, wasn't I? That $25,000 unsigned letter of agreement, for example; wasn't that a solid indication of Susskind's need?

"The point is, we think we have come up with the *true* account of the Black Sox Scandal," Brogger went on. "We think that the Carrolls' script is the more accurate version of what happened."

Here, he withdrew a sheet of paper from his attaché case and offered it to Storke. "Look at these references, Bill. It's a list of all the sources the Carrolls used in research. All very distinguished. And many of them tell it differently than what Eliot had written."

Storke glanced at the sheet, then looked at me. I nodded and he handed it across his desk. I immediately saw that it was an extensive bibliography of baseball histories, books, magazine articles, newspaper files, the works, a highly padded list they could not possibly have read in toto in the short time they had to work in. I had to laugh at the list, since many of the titles made little or no reference to the Scandal, anyway. I knew them all, of course. They were all part of my own sports library. What amused me, however, was the extent to which this was blatant eyewash. In fact, based on my reading of the script, it seemed to me appalling that Brogger should acclaim the Carroll script for its validity. Whatever it was as a television drama, it certainly was not a piece of history.

Again, however, I said nothing. I handed the bibliography back to Storke and returned to the davenport.

It was Storke's turn again.

"Well, Eliot has read the script, at my request, and has told me he has great reservations about its accuracy."

"What Eliot considers accurate is a subject of some debate, Bill," Brogger asserted.

"He *told* us he fictionalized," Diana repeated.

At this point, I confess to a flash of anger. They had volunteered to employ a gross distortion, then repeated it with such emphasis as to make it sound valid.

Storke looked at me. "Would you care to comment, Eliot . . . ?"

I thought about how to answer, for this was really the kind of thing best discussed at length, scene by scene, evaluating the thrust of the script as well as the so-called facts. But this was hardly the time and place for such a confrontation.

"I acknowledge that I don't have any lock on history. All historical events can be interpreted from varying points of view. The best I can say here is that I spent two years on the book, where Sidney and his son spent two weeks. I talked with the characters in the script. Abe Attell, for one. Those meetings between Attell and Arnold Rothstein that Sidney writes about—in fact, those scenes consume over half the screenplay—they're based on the faulty premise that the two were in it together. It just wasn't so. There never were such meetings. Attell manipulated the 1919 Series fix without Rothstein, and you won't find it mentioned otherwise in *any* of the titles listed on the Carrolls' bibliography."

I let that sink in, then added a quick bit of icing to the cake: "Sidney has Rothstein and others calling Attell 'Abie.' Well, nobody called Attell 'Abie.' Attell was one of the greatest fighters who ever lived, and he was called 'Champ.' And Attell never called Rothstein 'Arnie.' Nor did anyone else. Rothstein was known as 'A.R.' or, more intimately, 'Arnold,' but never 'Arnie.' " More silence. "I know it's a small thing," I added, "but indicative of Sidney's distance from the material."

Storke waited to see if I cared to continue. I did not. If they wanted a thorough critique, it would be for Sidney Carroll's benefit—and not as an adversary.

"Well, I'd say we had a problem," Storke went on. "I'd like to go ahead with this project. IBM is definitely interested, NBC equally so. But I'm not going to push the button until we get together with Eliot—sit him down with Sidney and work this thing out. It can only improve, and that's what we're all shooting for . . . the best show possible."

And so it was determined. I walked out of Storke's office with the three TA's, and we chatted briefly in the anteroom. Brogger was not particularly pleased with the prospects, a fact that bothered me.

"You're not demanding 'script approval,' are you, Eliot?" he asked, lending an ominous power to the phrase. "Because there's no way we could grant you that."

Since I had not signed the $25,000 agreement, I supposed he had reason to wonder what I was really after. If I had signed it and taken the money, we both knew how powerless I would be to do anything. Indeed, everyone from Storke on down knew that. The minute I signed that piece of paper, TA could do whatever they wanted. There would be no revisions; the show would go on as is.

"I'm interested in one thing, Fred," I replied, "an accurate script."

"But we've got an *excellent* script!" he said. "Everyone thought so. NBC, IBM, we were all set to go. I don't understand why you're doing this."

Well, there it was. The ultimate questioning of my motives—as though there were something devious behind my objections. I looked at Diana, whom I thought of as a friend.

"The script works, Eliot," she offered. "We all love you, you know that, but I don't think you're being sensible about this . . ."

Here, I snapped. Their approach was far too galling to let lie without comment. It was one thing for them to be tactical in Storke's presence; it was quite another that they believed their own fabrications. We were getting down to the nitty-gritty. No more guileful, calculating responses. I resorted to the hard-nosed, bottom-line, hard-assed truth.

"The script," I said, "is really a piece of shit!"

Now, it must be established that such verbiage, as horrible as it sounds, is nothing more than an uncomplimentary colloquialism. In the film business, it is used daily to describe a majority of the local product, rather accurately referring to all but the finest scripts around.

As it turned out, however, it was a phrase a lawyer would call "ill-advised," and I would pay a fearful price for having used it.

On Monday, April 12, four days after the meeting in Storke's office, Susskind returned from his vacation. When my phone rang that morning, I was not surprised to hear his voice.

He was clearly upset. He really could not understand what I was doing. He spoke for several minutes about what a fine screenwriter Sidney Carroll was and what a marvelous script they had from him. Everyone was tremendously enthusiastic about the project, he repeated. He regretted the unavailability of my book as a basis for the screenplay, but he could not see where I had any complaints, since I would be generously paid in spite of it.

"David," I said, "at the meeting it was decided that there ought to be changes."

He seemed not to hear me. He kept insisting that he was going to go ahead with the production whether I signed the agreement or not, once again mentioning that I could not have script approval; it was completely out of the question.

What stunned me was that there would be no revisions. He was determined to go with what they had. It was as if the big meeting with Storke had never happened! The way I read it, he had called Sidney—or Diana had—reporting on the meeting, and Sidney had demurred. Indeed, from his point of view, it was easy to understand. No doubt a writer of his stature had long since become involved in other work, and no writer willingly returns to finished projects for which they have been fully paid. To make changes in an accepted (bought) script to satisfy the author of a book he had not been permitted to use—and an apparently angry (irrational?) author to boot—was obviously not a pleasing prospect.

I told David that I would think it over and call him back. He reminded me that they were pressed for time. To air the show at World Series time, they would have to go into production no later than June 1. I said I knew that; I would call him no later than the following day.

It was a pretty kettle of fish, all right. There were too many ingredients in this potpourri that did not appear to belong, too many unexplained factors. What, really, was Storke's position at NBC? How much power did Susskind have in the overall decision? Could he really get a go-ahead without complying with Storke's requests?

An hour later, I called Storke.

"I have to talk to you again. In your office, Bill. Can you give me ten minutes . . . ?"

He was immediately agreeable.

Early the following morning I repeated the essence of my

conversation with Susskind, viz. that there was no opportunity for revisions, that David was prepared to go ahead with or without my signature.

"Can he do that?" I asked the $64 question. "Will NBC go ahead with his project if I refuse to sign?"

This stopped him, but only for a moment. "Let's face it, Eliot. If IBM wants to sponsor the show—and there is no question but that they are interested—David doesn't really need NBC. He can take it elsewhere. Any network would want it with a sponsor such as IBM . . ."

Meaning, no doubt, that NBC would too.

Ten minutes. That's all it took. I thanked him for his concern and left.

Depressed, I visited my lawyer friend, Steve Weinrib, whose office was a few blocks away. I had sent him the letter of agreement from TA to cover the possibility that I would sign it, hoping that at least a few of its terms might be revised in my favor.

"How does all this look to a lawyer?" I asked.

"Take the twenty-five thousand dollars," he said, pulling the revised agreement out for my signature.

"But don't I have *any* recourse? I mean, isn't there some way I could force Susskind to work this thing out?"

"You know something? You're crazy," he chided me. "It's just a lousy television show. Pfft, one night and it's gone."

"It doesn't have to be inaccurate."

"Take the money."

"I'll think about it," I said, leaving the unsigned paper on his desk.

I had lunch with another friend, Walter Bernstein, a highly talented, onetime-blacklisted screenwriter who had once written a number of exceptionally fine television dramas for Susskind during the trouble-filled 1950s when no one else would hire him. As a friend, he was sensitive to my problems; as a working professional, he was also acutely aware of the pitfalls.

We went back a long way together. In 1953 I was a neophyte

television writer and Walter was already an old pro. He had been encouraging and instructive when I needed guidance, and I was the better writer for it. When he was blacklisted, he came to me for support. Would I front for him? Though I hated the whole idea of it, we agreed that I had all the prerequisites of a perfect front. Since it was, perhaps, his last chance to make a living, I agreed. (Years later, Walter would write the story and screenplay for *The Front*, the Woody Allen film on blacklisting.)

So now I tossed the whole Susskind–Black Sox problem in his lap. (It was no strain; Walter enjoyed this sort of thing.) I waited for him to have a go at it.

"Well, I gather you're leaning toward your usual rebelliousness," he said.

"Wouldn't you, under the circumstances?"

He laughed. "I wouldn't get under your circumstances."

"Look, I'm confused."

"No kidding."

"Let's kick it around," I said. "For the sake of argument, let's say I'm refusing to sign."

"I'd say, tell me why. Could you convince that waitress that it makes sense to turn down twenty-five thousand dollars?"

"I doubt it."

"Convince me, then."

I thought about that. "I'm not sure I can convince myself. I guess I'd be turning down Susskind's deviousness—and the script that came out of it. I'm saying I don't want to be a part of it, that's all."

Even as I let this out, I sensed there was more, much more, more even than a criticism of the script itself. But I didn't know what was bothering me. Everything had become so confused, so much energy had been expended in gibberish and false issues and legal nonsense, somehow I'd lost contact with the essence of my motivations. I tried to explain all this to Walter, hoping that out of the stimulation the truth would emerge.

"It seems to me, El, you may be letting yourself get sucked in. You always need a cause. That's you. It's like your books, almost all of them; they're about some poor schnook who battles impossible forces and ends up getting the shit kicked out of him. They're marvelous, but what chance does he have?"

"He learns something. He comes out ahead in the long run."

"Okay, okay, but I'm wondering about you. Is this whole mess a reaction to something else? Something that has nothing to do with Susskind? Think about that. It happens to all of us, you know. We get fed up with all the shit in our lives. You especially. You have a continuing need to make a statement. You feel you're betraying something if you don't. Are you using Susskind just to make that kind of stand?"

"So what? Suppose I am. What's wrong with that?"

"Nothing. Except you're screwing yourself out of twenty-five thousand dollars."

"Walter, that script stinks!"

"So what else is new?"

"I don't want to let them get away with that script."

He shook his head, strongly in protest.

"What's the big issue? It's not venal, is it?"

"No, it's not venal. It's just warped."

"Take the money," he said. "Your position is clean. No one will condemn you for taking the money . . ."

Take the money. Take the money. Unquestionably, it was the sine qua non of survival in the entertainment business. An Eleventh Commandment, as it were, the sly sophism that resolved all problems. No one ever blamed anyone for taking the money.

It was a phrase that could wear a man down, whittling away his resistance until the wound was raw, the spirit infected. Inevitably, the mind would react, gradually modifying its stance, readily finding dozens of reasons to justify a shift. It might take a man half a lifetime to develop his powers to resist—and less than an hour to sell them out.

"As Ring said to the Committee, 'I'd hate myself in the morning.' "

"You wouldn't be hurting anyone. You'd get over it."

"It's not that simple."

"Complexity is the last refuge of a cop-out. It's *never* that simple."

"My point is, maybe I wouldn't get over it. Maybe when I saw the show I'd hate myself and you too."

"But it's just a lousy television show!"

I had to laugh, it was all so ludicrous. Nobody really cared. Make the deal, make the show, make the money, then take your chances with the critics, who didn't matter much anyway.

I remembered a scene, twenty-five years before, when television was in its relative infancy. One morning there was an urgent call to a mass meeting, and every television writer in the New York area (at the time, the center of TV production) was summoned to NBC's huge Studio Six (the setting for "Toscanini's NBC Symphony Concerts," no less), where the formidable head of the network, Sylvester "Pat" Weaver himself, wanted to speak to us. He marched to the podium with the austere look of a United States President about to convince a joint session of Congress to declare war, then he told us of a vision he'd had. The Bomb was about to fall on the great city, he said, all but obliterating the culture of the nation. He pleaded that those of us who somehow survived "would climb up out of that rubble and *re-create television.*" Believe it or not, that was the message. To the head of a network, television was to bring the light to a new civilization.

As it turned out, however, the Bomb that fell *was* television, and the networks themselves dropped it. The TV writers did not climb out of the rubble, we helped create it, a relentless slewing of puerile trash whose primary purpose was to sell junk that people didn't need and couldn't afford to buy.

Walter chided me. "There are also some pretty decent shows, and you know it."

"I suppose, but this won't be one of them."

"Okay. So you'll write an article exposing how it all came about. You'll have delivered your message and be twenty-five thousand dollars richer in the process. What's wrong with *that*?"

"Nothing," I said.

"So . . . ?"

"So, I agree."

"What? You're going to take the money?" He seemed astonished.

"Of course." I laughed. "I'm not crazy."

Obviously relieved, he shook his head with one last gesture of amused dismay. "That's what Chrlie Manson said."

I walked home with a feeling of benign resignation, preparing for my acquiescent phone call to Susskind. I would tell him, okay, I'll sign the agreement. I would take the money without shame. By God, I could even say I earned it.

In my apartment, I went straight to the telephone to make the call. I'd actually picked up the phone when I spotted the little red light on my answering machine, a reminder to play back any messages received during my absence. I returned the phone to its cradle, then pushed the appropriate button to rewind the tape, then another to set it rolling.

"Mr. Asseenof, my name is Bob Jagoda from IBM. I'm associated with media up here at Armonk, and we have the script on the Black Sox Scandal. There are a few questions about its accuracy, and I'd appreciate your calling me about this."

My first reaction was that this was a prank. Steve or Walter or any of a number of friends familiar with this running saga had gotten someone to make the call. Even the gross mispronunciation of my name was a ploy. There was no such person as Bob Jagoda. I was ready to bet that the number left was not IBM in Armonk but a gin mill in Brewster or a whorehouse in White Plains. All I had to do was sit for ten minutes and the phone would ring, a voice would laugh at me, no doubt calling me "Mr. Asseenof."

Nonetheless, I didn't wait. I called the number. It was IBM, and there was a real Bob Jagoda.

He was, in fact, extremely grateful for my cooperation. He told me that IBM was genuinely interested in the project, but had certain misgivings about the script. "Rereading your book, I noted a few rather important discrepancies. Then we wondered why your name is not credited on the title page of the script. Or a mention of your book, for that matter. I was hoping, Mr. Asseenof, that we might visit with you. I always try to discuss these things with the expert. We'd be more than happy to pay you an honorarium for your help in this matter . . ."

It was unbelievable. As they say, you couldn't write it any better. I could hardly speak for the suppressed laughter. I told him I'd be agreeable to visiting them in Armonk, and that an honorarium was not called for. He was delighted that I could come on the following morning; he would arrange a luncheon meeting with his boss, Chuck Francis, IBM's executive in charge of media.

I would save my call to David Susskind until later.

9.

The low-slung concrete building sat high above the parkway looking like an impregnable fortress. The approach from the vari-tiered parking area offered another formidable view, walks lined with thick shrubs expertly landscaped in a continuing sense of moving upward, level after level. Inside the vast glass-paneled lobby, I sat in thickly carpeted silence, looking out at stone courtyards with sturdy abstract statuary. The atmosphere was austere, forbidding, even ominous; for this was the home of the industrial giant, the International Business Machines Corporation.

I was engulfed by the trappings of wealth and power, by an incredible $15 billion a year in computers and typewriters, by the fifth largest corporation in America, by the legacy of the famed IBM president, Thomas Watson, capitalist par excellence, supermaterial-ist, arch-conservative, strict pragmatist, straitlaced religionist, ex-toller of Calvin Coolidge and Herbert Hoover, defender of the Fascist Benito Mussolini himself.

Bob Jagoda escorted me down an endless line of drab, indistinguishable cubicles, past diligent women secretaries fronting the white-shirted, short-haired executive males. I could not help but compare this setting with the curvy, silvered warmth of Talent Associates, with its long-haired, blue-jeaned young women in its inner offices, the sounds of laughter, controversy, enthusiasm.

Jagoda, manager of advertising services, was, himself, a cheerful, extremely pleasant man. His trim office reflected efficiency and business—so orderly, in fact, it seemed as if he had only recently settled in. Yet millions of dollars in annual promotional work went across his desk. Thirty-six television specials since 1972, quality productions designed to enhance the IBM image; shows such as "Eleanor and Franklin," "The Glass Menagerie," "The Belle of Amherst." Every Sunday, there was "Face the Nation."

He began by heaping praise on my book *Eight Men Out*, telling how he had first read it years ago, then again, recently, as the discussion of Sidney Carroll's script gave it urgency. His teenage son had also read it, and it made a strong impression on him, "opening his eyes to the ways of the world."

"I make it a policy to research these projects," Jagoda said. "Sometimes producers get careless with facts. We like to be as thorough as possible. It's such a simple thing to call an author and check things out . . ."

Then a colleague named Tony Franco came in, and together they began to talk about the script. They, too, did not go along with the guilty interpretation of Buck Weaver's involvement in the scandal. Jagoda could picture the wrath of older Chicago fans at the slander of a beloved hero. "Weaver was a victim, wasn't he? Wasn't he banned from baseball merely because he knew of the fix and refused to rat on his friends?"

Both men also protested against the oversimplification of the cover-up. "There's too much time spent in those meetings between Attell and Rothstein. Now why is that?" Jagoda asked.

I had listened quietly, nodding politely at a few of their critical comments, wondering exactly what function I could perform here. But when it became apparent that they were, in effect, challenging *me* on its content as though *I* were responsible, I realized there was no alternative but to tell them the entire story, just as I'd first told it to Bill Storke.

And just as Storke had been stunned, so was Jagoda.

I told him I regretted putting him in this rather uncomfortable position. After all, he was not a producer but an advisor at the sponsoring level.

"I was hoping there could be revisions in the script," I offered. "I'm glad to be here, if only to arrange for that; I mean, I really think it's important."

Jagoda nodded, told me to sit tight while he summoned Chuck Francis, the director of advertising at IBM, the executive with whom we were slated to have lunch.

Francis joined us in Jagoda's office a few minutes later, and I was asked to repeat the whole story to him. I did, and to the same shocked reaction.

"And we assumed you and your book were involved from the beginning," he said.

"Quite the opposite," I noted.

"But now you are?" he asked.

"Not quite. I'm here because I'd like to get the script revised."

"Well, doesn't Susskind now have the rights to your book? Don't you have some sort of contract with him?"

I explained that the option with another group was about to expire, that an agreement with Talent Associates was sitting in my lawyer's office, but that I had not signed it.

"Then you haven't been paid for any of this?" He seemed quite surprised.

"No. Not yet."

"Why haven't you signed it?"

"I'm concerned about the script, Mr. Francis," I said. "I'd like to think we could do a better show than this."

He eyed me skeptically for an instant. "I don't understand, Eliot. *You've refused to take the money?*"

He sounded so incredulous (or so I heard it), I did not know how to respond. He continued to regard me strangely, challengingly. I could hardly blame him for that. I'd had enough trouble convincing my own friends; how could I not give this executive from IBM the right to doubt me? Chuck Francis was a man whose responsibility it was to get shows on the air. He dealt with million-dollar budgets, was in contact with the highest levels of network executives and production companies (such as TA). Surely he did not make a practice of dealing with overwrought writers concerned with vague historical distortions.

But how to convince him? What could I say that could possibly make any sense?

I didn't know. I was a fish out of water in the first place, even more so in these offices than I was in NBC. At best, I have a difficult time functioning in such circumstances—not that light on my feet, as they say. I need time to think things out, to balance this wrinkle against that. By the same token, I am not a fast writer, seldom progressing more than two or three pages on a really good day. Though I was fully conscious that the success or failure of this excursion was likely to rest on what I would tell him, I was too fed up with all the preceding machinations to be guileful. For better or worse, I knew I would have to go with the way I felt.

"Mr. Francis, let me put it this way. This book, *Eight Men Out,* was a big thing for me to have done, and when it turned out so well, I was proud of it. Those ballplayers in the book, I met some of them. They were flesh and blood. I suppose I still care about them. This script doesn't portray them accurately. I can't get with that. It shouldn't be that way."

I stopped here, as much to take a breath as to gauge his reaction. His face revealed little beyond his confusion, or so I read it. I wasn't sure what to do. In my own confusion, I gave way to the need to continue.

"It's not just this one book. I've written quite a few books since then. Several have been bought by the movies, but the projects always seemed to turn out badly. I mean, the pictures weren't made at all, or they were terrible. Well, now it's *Eight Men Out.* Everyone tells me I'm making too much of this. They say, take the money and run. Well, I'm not sure what to do. The way I see it, this isn't just another yarn, it's a piece of history. Am I supposed to say, 'to hell with it,' and let another one of my projects turn into another piece of junk? I guess I mean, can't we say 'stop'; just this once, maybe, let's stop. Let's do it right or not at all."

Finally I came to a halt. Somewhere, in the midst of all that sophomoric holiness, I'd sensed my folly, but too late to control the momentum. I felt stupid, the more so for being in front of this group of corporate strangers.

I could hardly bear the silence that followed. I sat perfectly still, elbows resting on thighs, staring at Chuck Francis's polished black shoes.

"Well . . ." he began, not at all comfortably, to be sure. "We'd have to agree, that's a fine attitude. Really fine. I can promise you, we'll do everything we can to back your efforts. We're not creative people in this business. We don't produce the films. That's Susskind's job. But it seems to me this project would not be right without you. So let's see what we can do to make it come out right."

I took a deep breath, then let it out slowly. When I turned, Bob Jagoda was smiling broadly.

"Shall we go to lunch?" he suggested.

There were no martinis, no tall white-hatted chefs preparing Fettucini Alfredo in an executive dining room. We ate in the vast, classless, unsegregated IBM cafeteria, each of us bringing trays to a large table. We talked about the Black Sox Scandal and its meaning to America. Jagoda spoke compassionately of the eight ballplayers, seeing the tragedy through their eyes.

"What I learned from your book, Eliot, was the impact of their times, that they were helpless, really. There was nothing they could do to get free of it. They were playing ball and they loved it, but they must have hated Comiskey even more to do what they did."

Tony Franco referred to how good they were as a team. "Jackson, for example, would have become the best. They said he was the greatest natural hitter of them all. His averages were phenomenal. He hit .408 in his first full season. He never got as many hits as Cobb, but he was a far better hitter, and getting better every year. What a hitter he would've been had he been around for the lively ball!"

Chuck Francis was philosophical. "It must have been terribly upsetting for young Americans. Baseball is such a pure game. A marvelous game. It's hard to think of America without baseball, probably even more so in 1919 than today. Just think what people must have experienced when they heard that the World Series had been fixed!"

Bob Jagoda knew I'd played some professional ball and asked how far up the ladder I'd gone.

"Barely above the bottom rung," I replied. "For an outfielder, I didn't have the power. If it weren't for the war, I might have gone to Double A. I always managed to hit .300 but never in the style of 'Shoeless' Joe."

"Would you have kept trying anyway?" he asked. "Even if you knew it was hopeless?"

"When Buck Weaver pleaded for reinstatement all through the 1920s, he said he wanted to play so badly that he'd play for nothing. Well, that was me. You play that game for love. Even Babe Ruth was supposed to have said: 'What—you're gonna pay me to play this game?' "

They laughed, and suddenly I understood what this day was all about, why Jagoda had called me about the script in the first place. It was baseball. Whatever else we were, we had this one thing in common: one way or another, player, fan, observer, the game meant something special to each of us in a way no other game possibly could. It was far more than the four of us; one sensed the prevalence of baseball talk around these cafeteria tables in season, on all strata of IBM's power structure. A common denominator that was not untypical in America, and they could not but treat it with respect. In all my visits to TA over the years, through the half-dozen shows I'd written there, I'd never had such a conversation. I'd known dozens of its producers and directors, and though some must have played ball and others must have cared, no one cared enough to talk this way.

At IBM, however, baseball meant more than show business, and therein lay the difference.

When I left, I laughed all the way back to my car. That baseball itself had become the source of my victory was sheer poetry, and I drove back to New York wallowing in memories.

10.

At first memory, I was no more than seven years old, at summer camp in Massachusetts. Shy, insecure, it was said of me that I walked around like a kid who had just lost his dog. Then, one day I got into a ballgame, and with bases loaded I hit a towering shot over the center fielder's head for a game-winning home run. It was a drive that changed everything. I would never forget the sense of it, the overwhelming gratification in the power I'd generated, the exquisite sight of its flight, the exhilaration of running the bases. It must have been the day that the dour, maudlin look disappeared.

When I was thirteen, we moved out of New York City to Cedarhurst, Long Island. On a fine morning in late June, I set out on foot with my glove and spikes, knowing no one in this totally unfamiliar territory, hungering for the sight of a ball field. I walked for an hour, passing overgrown vacant lots, knowing there had to be kids playing ball somewhere. I would find them. All I had to do was to keep moving.

Then, zooming by at an intersection, I saw a boy on a bike, his mitt dangling from the handlebars. I hollered, but he did not hear. I took off after him, running to keep him in sight for as long as possible. Then I heard it before I could see it, the marvelous sound of bat on ball, and I turned a corner around a large house to see what had to be the most beautiful sight imaginable.

It was a magnificent little stadium. Dark green wooden grandstand that would seat maybe a thousand people. Fenced-in outfield with short right field. Bright green grass and a clean brown-dirt infield. Even the foul lines were shimmering white in the sun.

This was Cedarhurst Park, and it would become the center of my teenage life.

There were only seven kids on that field, including the bike rider who had led me there. Most of them seemed about my age, a few were older. They were dressed in old clothes, spikes, baseball caps. They were taking batting practice, outfielders running down every hit then throwing hard to second base, infielders taking ground balls and throwing to first for the simulated out. I watched for a few minutes, then put on my spikes and jogged to a vacant outfield position in left field. There were no introductions. I picked up names as I heard them. I ran down a long fly ball, turned, and threw leisurely to a relay man. Someone hollered, "Nice grab, Lefty," which would be my handle until much later in the day. When it seemed to be my turn to hit, I went in, grabbed the bat most suitable to my style, and took my cuts, but not before laying down two bunts, one to third, one to first. In spite of a nervous fluttering in my stomach, I hit well, enjoying the sight of the outfielders taking several steps back out of respect for my power.

After several rounds of hitting, having seen my first-baseman's mitt, there was no question but that I would play first during infield workout. They were all very good, deftly handling ground balls, throwing well. They executed double plays as though they'd been doing so for years. I had never played ball with such talented peers, nor felt closer to the game or more alive with my prospects than I did on that day.

And by the time we'd expended ourselves, four or five hours later, I'd made new friends, four of whom would be classmates through high school.

For the first time in my life I sensed a purpose. Because of them and what we had in common, I knew I would become a real ballplayer—the best I could possibly be.

Over that summer, baseball became a passion. More, it gave me a goal to shoot for. I wanted to be a professional ballplayer, an ambition I defiantly blurted out one Sunday at a large family gathering. If this was not blasphemy to my parents, it was because they tolerated such idiot outbursts as the braying of an overly romantic child. To them, life was to be lived within a well-circumscribed set of guidelines, the purpose being a legitimate quest for status and money in some highly respected vocation. My father and his father before him, together with my two uncles, had successfully manufactured boy's clothing for over fifty years—a business that was there for me to perpetuate. As a boy, I could think of nothing I would care to do less.

In high school (Lawrence High), the years revolved around spring and summer. With my friends, I talked baseball constantly. The game became a religious affiliation—not for the Dodgers or the Yankees, but for us. We were not coached. (The high school "coach" was a geometry teacher who didn't even know the Infield-Fly Rule.) We worked things out ourselves. We practiced time plays to pick runners off second base, double-squeeze plays with runners on second and third that scored both, delayed steals with runners on first and third that advanced both.

Above all, we practiced hitting. We would hit for hours, then talk about technique, analyzing our swings. At the age of fifteen, we already knew the dangers of overstriding and hitching and would constantly correct each other.

Meanwhile, I worked on special skills. I built a sliding pit in the backyard (behind the garage) and learned to slide equally well on both sides. I learned to bunt for base hits, not only down the third-base line, or the first-, but just behind the right-handed pitcher as his motion took him off the mound. I'd read that Ty Cobb would lay a sweater on a strategic spot between the mound and first base, then drop bunts on it time after time. I did that for as long as I could get someone to throw to me.

Baseball was an endless joy. For the long season, the only enemy was rain. Over the winter, there was never a day when I did not swing a bat, or hold it at arm's length to strengthen my wrists, or handle my well-oiled mitt for a few minutes of pounding.

There was no doubt that we were good. Four of us made the high-school varsity at the age of fourteen, twice winning divisional championships. I became team captain my senior year, hit .537, and was nominated for the World Telegram Award for the Outstanding High School Ballplayer in the New York Metropolitan Area. I was team captain again at Swarthmore College, also playing twilight semiprofessional ball in nearby Chester, Pennsylvania, sometimes changing uniforms (and names) in the car between games. It was at Swarthmore that I met the great pitcher for the Philadelphia A's of Connie Mack, George Earnshaw, who, in his fading years as a ballplayer, pitched Sunday ball for the New York Bushwicks. During the week, he would throw batting practice to us, mostly half speed, to keep his arm in shape. When I faced him, however, he would smile in recognition of my intensity, and would cut loose with his best stuff. I loved the challenge, muttering to myself, "Nothing gets by me! Nothing!" and I'd hit him, all right. Then he'd smile, and fool me with an off-speed breaking pitch.

"You're tough, all right," he said to me one afternoon. (This from a man who'd pitched to Ruth and Gehrig!) I'd never heard such a compliment before, and it rang in my ears for days, a continuing source of pleasure. We became friends, and I'd visit his home in Swarthmore (he was also fire chief at the time) and sit at his feet through occasional evenings, listening to him talk baseball.

Then, late in the spring, he asked me, "You want to play pro?"

"I'd thought about it some," I said with colossal understatement.

He smiled. "Jocko Collins wants to meet you," he said. Collins was head of the Phillies' farm system.

Earnshaw himself brought me in, and a few days later I suited up with the Phillies, my first and only appearance in a Big League uniform. I took batting practice, then replaced Art Mahan at first during infield workout. I wasn't nervous. It was all too much of a dream. Besides, this was the worst Phillies team in history.

During the summers, I played in a college league in New England that was run under Big League auspices to keep the best college ballplayers under professional tutelage without violating our amateur status. Almost all of us went on to play pro ball, and more than a few made it to the majors. Among them, a remarkably good ballplayer named Mickey Rutner, also from New York, who would later become important to my writing career.

The day I graduated from college, the Phillies signed me to a contract. My bonus was a glass of beer and a cheap cigar.

The two seasons of my professional career were a continuing joy. The prospect of playing seven or eight games a week, or actually living for baseball, seemed more rewarding than any previous baseball experience. It established a continuity that added professionalism to the game, and though my salary was never more than $100 a month, the size of the paycheck was less important than the fact of it.

It was a time of learning and self-appraisal. I came to understand my limitations as well as my talents, especially in the presence of ballplayers better equipped than I. I saw men my age hit with intimidating power, fielders whose throwing arms were far stronger than mine, others far swifter on the base paths. Undaunted, I continued to work at what talents I had, learning something more about the game each time out. Hitting became like a chess game, every pitcher representing a different rival. Years later, Yogi Berra would say, "I can't think and hit at the same time," but my own style was the opposite. I relied on thinking. On chilly nights, for example, long before batters used golf gloves, if you hit one off your fists you'd get a shock all the way to your armpits. As a result, pitchers would jam you, immobilizing your swing. I learned to anticipate that, to turn with the pitch and meet it out front. (I even got to be known as a cold-weather hitter.) I learned to watch whether a pitcher got tired in late innings, noting the length of his stride as he threw. If it was longer than before, he was rearing back too far, working to put a little extra on his fast ball. At that point he was likely to throw fewer curve balls, and his fast ball would eventually come in letter high—which was exactly where I liked it. Sometimes, when a pitcher was throwing well, I would try to hit the pitch he wanted me to hit, that low-and-away curve ball, knowing it was his best. So I'd wait for it, then punch it to left. I'd hear stories about great hitters who needed to hate pitchers in order to hit them. Al Simmons, for example, would wave his bat and glare at the mound as though he had murder in his heart. I never felt that way. I always came to the plate smiling. I think I loved it all so much, the pitcher was out there just to give me the chance to hit.

Though I was a good ballplayer, I knew I would never be good enough. Just being around hitters like Mickey Rutner made it obvious. Local sportswriters, however, aware of my higher batting average, rated me better than Rutner, but it only exposed their ignorance. "You really look like a ballplayer," they'd say. I suppose I did, but I knew it didn't mean a thing.

So I played for joy, if not for ambition. The long, battering bus rides after night games, the inadequate lights, grubby locker rooms, sleazy hotel rooms, terrible food, low pay . . . nothing bothered us, for we were playing ball. Some managers were destructive and cruel. Other clubs jockeyed with a barrage of anti-Semitic obscenities that eventually fanned the prejudices of the spectators. It was, in many ways, a hate-ridden, competitive world, but in the end, the game was the thing, the only thing. As Mickey Rutner would put it: "Fuck 'em all, big and small." We were there because we loved the game. Baseball was played with a bat and a ball and a glove, not with a mouth. It was all out in the open, what you could do or couldn't. Any baseball man could see it. Not just the statistics, but everything. Speed, timing, throwing, hustle. There were politics and prejudice and favoritism about who went up and who didn't, and the slave system under which all professional ballplayers lived was riddled with tragic inequities. Everyone knew it. But when you were playing, nothing could take away the joy.

One summer the Phillies sent me to their Class-C farm club in Wausau, Wisconsin. The playing manager was an ex–Big League third baseman named Wally Gilbert, broken down at forty with an expanding waistline and a propensity for too much whisky. In the late innings of a close game, I was on first with one out when Wally came to bat and gave me the hit-and-run sign. The third baseman was playing deep, protecting the line against a sharply pulled extra-base hit that might permit me to score. I took off on the pitch as Wally laid down a perfect bunt, and as the third baseman made a desperate try to throw him out, I rounded second on high, for third was being left unguarded. As it turned out, it was perfect, absolutely perfect. I stood on the base like a king of the hill, smiling across the diamond at Wally, safely on first, breathing heavily from his sprint, hands on hips, cap down low over his eyes. He met my eye and nodded, a routine complimentary nod from one pro to another. He was over twice my age, but he did not patronize. Though we had never practiced the play—nor even discussed trying it—he knew I would get there. And that's what made it so perfect.

I'd been accustomed to hearing people at home say that I was a fool to play ball. I'd never make it to the Big Leagues, they'd tell me. My college education, the cum-laude degree, all that high-cultured energy was being wasted. I should be pursuing a real career, settling down, making money. Baseball was for farm boys, etc., etc. At the time, I didn't know how to answer them. It wasn't until I joined them, years later, that I realized how wrong they were. What did they ever do that was more beautiful than that moment in Wausau? Produce trashy television shows? Sell deodorants? As I write this, a thirty-nine-year-old ex–Big-League pitcher named Jim Bouton has given up a lucrative broadcasting career, mortgaged his home, and destabilized his family for the unlikely but exquisite challenge of trying to make it back to the biggies. *He* knows where the beauty is.

11.

When I came back from Armonk and IBM, I immediately called Bill Storke at NBC to report on the meeting.

It stunned him, all right, but I could not judge his reactions.

"Have you told David?" he asked, not without a trace of anxiety.

"I'm going to call him now."

David, of course, was wholly unprepared for this. Anticipating my call of acquiescence, he could hardly be blamed for his distress at hearing the opposite.

"What right do you have going up there?" he snapped.

"I told you, they called me," I replied.

"I don't believe that. You called them, just like you called NBC."

Nor, I suppose, could I blame him for that, but I was not about to argue the matter. I had a purpose here, and I pursued it.

"Look, David, what this is all about is that television script. It's inaccurate, and I'm trying to help get it revised. Bill Storke agrees with me and now so does Chuck Francis. Do you want to hear what I have to say about it . . . finally?"

Late the following afternoon, I was in Susskind's office, carrying a copy of "Say It Ain't So, Joe," replete with extensive notes, a copy of my book, and assorted commentaries. Diana Kerew was waiting for me, ready with note pad, I was pleased to see. In the anteroom of David's office, he was on the phone, standing by a secretary's desk: "Nobody wants to see a fifty-year-old man suffering in loneliness," he was saying. "Why not make it a young love story with a happy ending. Give people a chance to look at something pleasant."

I had to agree with that, anyway.

He came in, looking considerably more harassed than I'd ever seen him. He excused Diana. He said he thought it best to talk to me alone.

I sat down on the davenport, laid my briefcase on the coffee table, ready to work. David was moving across the floor, a step or two this way, then that, fumbling with a folder of typewritten notes. He sat down at last and began to read. First, he read me Diana's interpretation of what had happened with the project over the preceding months. Then he skipped to a comparable analysis from Ron Gilbert, periodically inserting his own recollections. Apparently he'd had them all write memos on the chain of events leading up to the current crisis, a compilation of self-serving comments that made a heavy out of me.

I made no reply, but opened my briefcase to go to work on the script.

"Well, isn't that the way it happened?" he asked. "Doesn't it jell with the facts?"

I really didn't know what to say. How could one respond to a quote from Diana: "When I told Eliot of the new project that did not include his book, he didn't seem at all disturbed." Or that Sidney Carroll claimed that I'd made a date with him and broken it. Or that Ron Gilbert said something about how I agreed to sign, then refused. These things were true as far as they went; they just didn't go far enough. But I was not there for the purpose of defending myself or attacking them.

"The script, David . . ."

"What did I do wrong?" he kept asking me. "I *tried* to get the rights to your book. You told me you could get them. But you couldn't, Eliot. So what was I supposed to do!"

How could I answer that? His lawyers told him he could go to the public domain, so that's what he did. But since that would destroy my equity in my book, what did he expect *me* to do? Didn't he think I might object? Didn't his action automatically put me in an adversary position? Now that his own pigeons had come home to roost, couldn't he at least face up to that reality?

And, at long last, couldn't we talk about that bloody script?!

I said that to him. I said I didn't care to comment on that other garbage. I kept opening the pages of Sidney's script, tapping the annotated margins with my pen.

"I don't know, I don't know," he sighed. "I think this project is doomed," and he stared at me with an accusatory shaking of his head. "You should never have gone to Storke," he went on. "If only you hadn't done that. You should have come directly to me. We could have settled everything. I would have given you the money . . ."

I winced in frustration. There were so many ramifications to all these irritating tidbits, how could I make sense of it?

"David," I said feebly, "I did go to you. I called you repeatedly, but you weren't reachable. As for the money, I didn't own the rights. How could I take any money from you when I didn't own the rights?"

He didn't seem to understand, and I was not going to pursue it. A moment later, however, he came up with a whole new tack.

"Eliot," he said, "do you think you can work with Sidney?"

It was incredible. Victory can come sneaking around corners just as easily as it comes soaring in with a fanfare of trumpets.

Then, even before I could respond, he snatched it away. "The question is, could Sidney work with you after you called his script 'a piece of shit' . . ."

"What! You told Sidney I said that?"

"Well, he's heard it, all right."

The thought enraged me, especially since it seemed so typical of the whole mess. Little chunks of poisoned shrapnel exploding in all directions. If I'd said it, it was in anger at Diana and Fred Brogger, certainly not for Sidney's ears.

"Look, David, I came here to talk about the script. You obviously don't want to talk about it. I'd be happy to discuss it with Sidney. That's what I've wanted to do for weeks."

Suddenly resolute, he turned to the telephone and finally made contact with Sidney in Boston. Yes, he would meet with me. He would come in on the following Monday.

I agreed, and we both felt better about that.

"He's a fine man, a first-rate writer," he said. "He shouldn't have to do this, you know . . ."

I knew. I'd been a bad bad boy, but Susskind and now Sidney were graciously willing to let bygones be bygones. He smiled reassuringly, even offered his hand in a warm, willing handshake. I assured him I was just as eager as he to get this project on the road. I would do everything I could to help. I told him how pleased I was to meet with Sidney, finally, that only constructive things would happen when a writer of his stature would be permitted to use the material in my book.

As a matter of fact, I added, I would prepare a set of scenes for

Sidney that would correct the inaccuracies; he would no longer be left with the skimpy pickings of the public domain. As a result, I felt sure that the script would be aces, that it would please David, Storke at NBC, and the gang at IBM.

And for all this extra work on my part—which I, too, should not have to do—I thought David should pay me.

"I think twenty-five hundred dollars is a fair figure," I said. "Wouldn't you agree?"

I know. I should have insisted he write me a check then and there, if only just to watch him wriggle out of it. But I didn't. I didn't because I refused to make an issue out of money in this project. Besides, he seemed not to hear me.

There was nothing further to discuss, so I put my materials back in my briefcase and left.

12.

Having made the commitment to Susskind, I worked hard that weekend. I reread Sidney's script. I reread my own book. Working carefully, I plucked a number of key scenes that would fit into Sidney's structure and corrected those distortions I had found so grating.

Janet was amused at the intensity of my efforts.

"Do you ever get the feeling that you've gone absolutely and completely bananas?" It was less a question than a comment, of course.

"Masturbation is *not* a sign of insanity."

"Right. I was only wondering why you were working so hard."

"Because it's *there*," I mumbled.

Why, indeed.

Sure, I knew. No one would even read what I was writing, much less pay me for it. Sidney was probably not even going to show up for the meeting. I'd been a victim of my own inflated enthusiasm, and I felt that sickening sensation that I'd been here before—the sure sign of another defeat. It was all so preposterous I had to laugh.

" 'Ridi, Pagliaci,' " she sang.

On Monday morning, I rallied my sagging spirits, pleased with the weekend's work. I walked all the way down to Susskind's office, full of hope at the prospects of a rapprochement. And, sure enough, there was Sidney Carroll, a big, friendly man, to bolster my enthusiasm. It did not bother me that he had obviously arrived earlier, presumably for a quick preliminary conference with Susskind. (Indeed, they were huddled together as I arrived.) David introduced us, turned over his spacious office for our convenience. Diana was there with her notebook in hand, but this time it was I who asked that she be excused. If I was going to be blunt with my opinions, it would hardly be politic to subject a writer of Sidney's stature to the possible embarrassment of her presence.

And so, at long last, we began. There was no discussion of our divergent positions, no suggestion of animosities, no sign of re-crimination. We were going to talk script.

I opened the black plastic cover of Sidney's "Say It Ain't So, Joe," and began working from my marginal notes. Sidney laid a legal pad and pen on the coffee table before him, then sat back on the davenport, his right arm stretched across its back. I explained that the corrections I wanted to make were of varying textures, some of minor importance, others basic distortions of history. On page 4, for example, Ed Cicotte was not "the fastest pitcher in the American League," he was famous for what they called a "shine ball," wherein he would rub the baseball with a concealed emery cloth, thereby creating a knuckle-ball–type reaction. (He was, in fact, nicknamed "Knuckles" as a result.) Nor was Happy Felsch "the best center fielder in baseball"; Tris Speaker was. Or, on page 14, Buck Weaver was not "money hungry," nor did he ever agree to participate as a fixer. On page 25, the opening game was not on Monday but on Wednesday; the World Series never opens on a Monday. On page 30,

Arnold Rothstein is quoted as having the betting odds at 5–2. No one ever got 5–2. The *best* odds on the White Sox before the fix leaked out were 10–7.

It was the sort of stuff baseball fans cared about. Networks would receive annoying letters. There was really no excuse for that . . .

Somewhere around this point, I noted that Sidney was neither taking notes nor showing more than polite attention.

"This doesn't interest you?" I asked.

He was respectful of my knowledge, but unconcerned for such detail. "Eliot, I'm a dramatist, not a historian," he said. "Facts have no great importance. The drama is the thing. I really don't care very much about facts. I read them, try to absorb them, then extract the essence. It's the drama that counts . . ."

"Does drama *have* to be at the sacrifice of the truth, Sidney? Why let the facts get out of hand when you can have it both ways?" Then I leaped into the breach, attacking the important distortions, like his interpretation of Buck Weaver's involvement. "You've got Weaver bargaining for money, you've got him throwing ballgames. He never did that, Sidney. Never."

He shrugged off my indignation. "My son David's research had him involved," he countered.

"What research?" I cried out, more strident than diplomatic, immediately conscious that I'd be driving this discussion up a blind alley with my abrasiveness. After all, he was not a historian, he was a dramatist. It suited his dramatic needs to have Weaver involved. He didn't care about Weaver. Weaver was just another puppet. Besides, as Fred Brogger had said, "There is still a big mystery surrounding what happened in the Black Sox Scandal."

Respectful of my earnestness, however, Sidney suggested that perhaps I was too close to the material, that it meant too much to me. I replied that until I'd read his script I hadn't read my book in ten years.

"Look, Sidney . . ." I said softly, moderating my style, "I want to open the door for you. I've taken a number of scenes from my book that you can insert into your structure. I really think they'll make your characters come alive. They'll give the story more scope as well as accuracy."

I handed him my notes, and he thanked me. He glanced at them quickly, then laid them down. I didn't know what else I expected him to do, though I kept hoping he would do some probing of his own. We sat quietly for a moment while I struggled to come up with some new approach to revitalize my flagging spirits.

What I felt was his apathy. It was normal enough. He had done his work, and it had been well praised and paid for. Then I had come along to make trouble. No doubt he was involved in new projects, his creative juices flowing elsewhere. Why should he bother with rewrites, expecially in a sticky situation such as this?

Obviously, then, there was nowhere to go in this meeting. We rose from our respective davenports, collected our papers, and prepared for departure. It was all very friendly, of course. He even confessed to me that he'd read my book and thought highly of it. He also indicated his sympathy for whatever troubles had been inflicted upon me because of this situation. I told him that I hoped he would find my contributions helpful, that he should feel free to phone me at any time. He thanked me again, and I left. The last I saw of him as I turned to the elevator, he and David Susskind were chatting together.

13.

Whatever, I was back on the ropes again. I descended the thirty-three floors to the lobby feeling defeat wriggling through my blood like super-resistant gonococci. When the elevator door opened, I hungered for sunlight, even the Third Avenue version of it.

But I saw—indeed, he was coming right at me—one of the ten most objectionable people I'd ever met. I'd long since forgotten his name, but I knew him. The walk alone would give him away. Tall, but slouched. Loose-limbed and gangling like an awkward teenager.

Even the way his attaché case knocked against his right leg was familiar. He was, or pretended to be, a moviemaker.

He saw me and stopped, the old long-time-no-see greeting. How had I been? What was I up to? He kept insisting that we have a drink together, immediately, for he had a marvelous project for which I would be the perfect writer, tapping his attaché case to prove it, then making me squirm as his hand clutched the inside of my arm.

Though I quickly brushed him off, meeting him again at that moment was the punctuation mark on my defeat.

When I first confronted him, he was the defeat itself. It was in Cuba, no less. May 1959, a few months after I'd returned to New York, recently divorced, and far from Hollywood. I was hungry for an action to sink my teeth into, the more challenging the better, when my friend Harvey Orkin, a writer turned agent, called to ask if I cared to go to Cuba. It was barely five months after Castro had come to power; how could I resist? "Some cockamamy film director is having trouble with a script he's shooting. All I know is, Lon Chaney, Jr., is in it."

By five-thirty that same afternoon, I was met at the Havana airport by this same director, a frazzled script in his nervous hands, and we were immediately en route to the National Palace for a meeting with Cuban officials. The problem, as he explained it, was Castro's insistence that a Cuban writer be employed, especially since the film dealt with the Revolution. Unfortunately, however, the writer was totally inept, a fact that became quickly apparent as I read the first few scenes as we drove. My function was to convince the government officials that I could collaborate with this man on rewrites.

A moment later, we walked into a smoky office, and I looked into the bearded face of Fidel Castro himself. It so startled me, I broke out laughing.

"Saludo," I said for the first time in my life.

"Bueno . . ." said Fidel, offering his hand.

We shook, and he pulled a cigar from his fatigue pocket, handed it to me.

72

It was unbelievable. The whole meeting was unbelievable. The Cuban writer, the head of the newly formed government film department, two or three others . . . a lot of loud Spanish was spoken, none of which I understood. I sat there quietly, smoking the magnificent cigar, trying to avoid staring at Castro. They finally talked to me in English, having determined how the Cuban writer and I would rewrite the scenario. The ever-smiling director was quick to agree, turning to me for approval, nodding insipidly, eyes pleading. It was a moment of consummate absurdity. To be the Main Man in this battle over a script I had hardly read—dealing with the Revolution, no less—was crazy enough. In the presence of Fidel Castro, it was sheer madness. Further, that I should be brought before one of the most dynamic political figures in the world by a spineless, insipid fool could only add to the madness.

Then, Fidel was looking at me.

"So . . . ?" he asked.

"No," I replied, "I'm very sorry, but I can't work that way. I must work alone."

The director gasped. Someone translated my refusal. The Cuban writer paled, stared first at me, then at Castro. Castro glanced at his cigar, puffed, then rose. He muttered something to his minister, then pointed toward me, nodding in approval.

For reasons I could not understand, I had won. I would do the rewrites alone.

Four weeks later, I was rolling dice at the Hotel Capri (gambling had not yet been outlawed in Cuba) when I saw Castro again, wandering through the casino in green fatigues with a few distinguished-looking guests. I could not help staring at him, eager to catch his eye in the vague hope that he might remember me. He did. He smiled, and stepped over to the crap table.

"So, how is the film?" he asked.

I explained that my work was finished but they were still shooting. I was sorry to report that it had been chaotic. This was quickly translated for him, and he shrugged. I was relieved that it didn't appear to bother him.

"You are a baseball player, no?" he asked.

I almost pissed my pants. Had he checked me out—or had the unpredictable Harvey Orkin dispatched this piece of information via diplomatic pouch?

"Poco," I replied—not bad, not good—the only modest word in Spanish I could think of.

He smiled. I could see that he liked me, a thought that was more than I could cope with.

"Go . . . See our country," he said. "Havana is not all of Cuba." I nodded.

"Pinar del Río is very nice," he said. "Just go."

Pinar del Río was, indeed, very nice. I was the only American there, and it couldn't have been nicer. With my Berlitz pocket book of Spanish phrases, I worked my way through the hot streets with laughing children following me, drank Bacardi Cuba libres for fifteen cents, marvelous demitasse for five, and smoked the best cigars in the world for a quarter. After a week, I was even asked to play *beisbol* for a local fruit-canning plant in a twilight game, fully uniformed and vigorously cheered whenever I caught routine fly balls in the outfield. I received two job offers to teach English, had one proposal of marriage from a young widow. They were ten days full of friendliness and fun, the most enjoyable time I'd ever spent on foreign soil.

Over a year later, I noticed ads for a new film called *Barbudos* ("Bearded Ones"), starring Lon Chaney, Jr., allegedly depicting the horrors of Communist tyranny under Castro. I was appalled to see that it was, indeed, the film I had worked on, corrupted by the director into a grotesque counterrevolutionary piece of trash, good guys turned into bad guys, scenes emasculated and butchered, others spliced and distorted, dialogue added on the sound track. Times had changed since 1959, and the chameleon director had reconstructed the scenario to suit them. I watched this putrid movie in a wash of tears, wondering how in hell it had gotten to this point. Unable to sleep, I typed a long letter to Fidel expressing my pain at what I had seen. Early the next morning I walked to the post office to see if it might be properly mailed. For weeks, I half expected to get an answer, but of course I never did.

It was March 1961, and history had taken us to the Bay of Pigs.

14.

It came as no surprise that no $2,500 check arrived from Talent Associates. A day or so after our meeting, Sidney called to report that he had read my notes and was thinking about the revisions. It was a friendly call, and I was encouraged by it.

Hardly a day later, however, Susskind called and reversed my mood.

"Eliot, Eliot . . ." he began in plaintive tones, "I don't know what to do . . . ," and I knew immediately we were back to square one. "I don't know what I've done that's so wrong. I've spent a lot of money and effort to get this project going. I put a fine writer on it, had new research done. I had the whole production ready, then you came and fouled it up by going to NBC and IBM. You took it on your own to damage my equity worth almost a million dollars! Now I'm ordering you to desist damaging that equity. I warn you, I will serve papers on you. What I want is your cooperation, not your objections. You can cooperate by signing the agreement and taking the twenty-five thousand dollars. You can have whatever credit on the screen you wish. . ."

(I thought, How about "Say It Ain't So, Joe" by Sidney and David Carroll, NOT based on the book *Eight Men Out* by Eliot Asinof?)

I made no reply.

"I don't know how much money you have, Eliot," he went on, "but I'm going to sue you for all of it if you persist in this stand!"

I almost exploded with laughter. We were so far apart, any discussion seemed absurd. In such moments, a bevy of prospective

75

arguments run through one's mind, but they dissolve into useless verbiage. I simply replied that I'd think about it. He said he had no more time, that he had to get the production rolling. He told me to call him at home if necessary, then gave me his private number. I promised that I would.

I reached Steve Weinrib, attorney, the next day, to report the threat. He laughed. "What's he going to sue you for, *not* signing?" But a day later, Steve called me back, reporting a phone conversation he had had with Ron Konecky, attorney for Talent Associates. He now believed that there might very well be a suit against me based on my harassments to Susskind's equity in the show, precisely as he had threatened. No doubt Susskind could not win such a suit, but I'd have to undertake costly legal fees to defend myself, and he reminded me of the imbalance of Susskind's corporate resources in comparison to mine.

His advice: "Sign! Take the money!" Then, with a burst of laughter: "What in hell is going on inside your head anyway!"

By this time it might be assumed, even by me, that I no longer really knew. The possibility of a lawsuit was a whole new wrinkle. I wasn't at square one; I had passed it going the wrong way, moving full speed back to the doghouse. But even that seemed too absurd. How could he possibly sue me? What had I done that could possibly be deemed litigable? Surely Susskind's lawyers would have to advise him that he had no case.

Indeed, the way I saw it, Susskind's suit was merely a bluff, a threat to induce my compliance.

Then again, I could be rationalizing my own prejudices. Was I not, in fact, being perverse? Why *didn't* I take the $25,000? I certainly needed it. Nor were there likely to be alternatives to this sale, for if I turned down this final offer, there would doubtless be "a cloud over the property" that would blot out any future interest in my book. All litigations were killers. *Eight Men Out* would become dead, and I would lose the battle, the war, the money, everything.

When I returned home the next afternoon, I entered to the full, rich sound of my stereo, with Janet singing "I Could Have Danced

All Night" solidly behind Julie Andrews—almost indistinguishable, I thought.

"Catchy tune," I said as they finished. "What is it?" And I went for the bottle of Scotch, noting that I'd been drinking more than usual during this siege.

"You look like the Man in the Iron Mask," she said.

"I guess I need a shave."

I raised my glass in a toast, then nipped away.

"He called about an hour ago," she said.

"Who?" I quipped.

"Who? Him, that's who."

"Did he say what he wanted?" Another laugher.

"Shit," she replied.

She, too, laughed, but there was too much pain, and it stuck in her throat. I was careful not to look up at her, aware that this mess was starting to get to her.

"You sing real nice," I said.

"Damned good waitress, too," she added.

I flipped my hand, palm down, palm up, in a *comme ci comme ça* gesture.

"What are you going to do?" she finally asked.

She was staring at me now as though she might find the answer in the way I sipped my drink. I stopped that by staring back, opening a toothy smile that was all artifice and a yard wide.

"Sometimes I think you're actually enjoying all this," she said.

I'd thought of that too. For all the madness and frustration, for all the waste of time and energy, there was something happening that sparked me.

"Is that so bad?"

"Depends . . ." she said. "It's bad if you're in it *because* you like it. It's good if you like it in spite of being in it."

"Which am I?"

She shrugged. "Maybe a little of both."

I clicked ice cubes in my glass, sipping Scotch and musing. What was I going to do?

All of a sudden, I had to decide. The game was finally coming to an end, and whatever followed would be real. Depending on which way I decided, the reality would take on a new dimension.

I needed this the way I needed another navel.

It left me with that stupid feeling again. Or that feeling of stupidity—that I was a colossal ass.

If you can't hit curve balls, you shouldn't play in the Big Leagues.

How did one make such decisions? There was nothing to think over anymore, for all that had been done many times over. If one bothered to think at all, more than likely it would only serve as a rationale for what had already been decided for some totally irrational reason.

Could I actually say, "Yes, I'll take the twenty-five thousand dollars," now that I'd finally won the power to stop the show after saying no when I didn't?

If I submitted now, what was the point of the fight in the first place?

Ah, but there's a new ingredient, came the return argument: the threat of a lawsuit if I don't submit.

Again, was that real? How real?

Could I honestly say it frightened me? Intimidated me?

If so, was I not the ultimate sucker, the patsy who could be made to submit merely by the threat of litigation. If someone says "Kiss my ass, Asinof, or I'll sue!" do I kiss?

But wait. No one would say I kissed ass. Everything but. Besides, there's twenty-five big ones coming to me, etc., etc., and all I have to do is sign my bloody name!

It frequently happens that the last one to advise you is the final determinant, purely because he is the last. For that reason, I did not ask Janet for her opinion, knowing that she might hold herself responsible if the decision turned out badly. I would do it on my own and without magnifying its importance. It *was* just a television show, and what difference did it make one way or the other? To get down to the real bedrock, *how much did I really care?*

I poured myself another shot, this time without ice or soda, thinking maybe insouciance would supply the answer. I was weary of the problem—like a second-rate chess player dizzily trying to pit his prospective moves against the countless variables of his opponent. A copy of *Eight Men Out* was on the adjacent end table, and I reached for it, flipping through pages at random, remembering this scene or that and how I had chased it down, finally settling my eyes on the pictures in the center of the book.

There was Joseph Jefferson Jackson, his eyes barely visible behind the dark shadow cast by the peak of his cap, staring into the camera with a ferocity pitchers must have found completely intimidating. And Eddie Cicotte in a short haircut, polka-dotted bow tie to blend with a light, dotted suit, his troubled face poised on the brink of a smile. And Buck Weaver in uniform, boyish, open-mouthed, staring intently at what seemed like a distant fly ball. And Oscar "Happy" Felsch, square-jawed, good-looking, his lips curling at the ends like one containing laughter. I lingered on Felsch, remembering that afternoon we had spent together, the bottle of Scotch I'd brought dwindling after hours of talk. At the end, his wife had come in to check on him, for he was ill with cancer, and hearing the pleasure in his voice, retreated to a corner of the room to listen, allowing us a few minutes more, I supposed. We had talked about the world he'd lived in, the 1919 experience and the way it had hurt him, and when he saw her, he raised the last toast to her.

"I shoulda knew better . . ." he'd said. "I just didn't have the sense I was born with."

"It's all right, dear," she comforted him. "It don't matter no more."

He drank up, then looked back at me, trying to smile, but for the first time that afternoon, it didn't really work.

Then he mumbled something I didn't hear.

"What?" I asked, leaning toward him.

"It matters . . ." he said. "It still matters."

Now, I put the book down in a wash of sentiment, boozed up enough to wallow in it. I knew the dangers of making decisions in that condition, but it didn't bother me. The curious part was the realization that there really never had been much of a doubt as to what I would do. I had only to riffle through Carroll's teleplay again to be reminded of its failings. The entire experience with Susskind seemed all of a piece. It was, as everyone had said, just a TV show, a commodity just like the beer-tire-bank-deodorant it was made for. To sell the product, the show became as meretricious as the commericals that would chop it up. It was important only to its maker and for its salability. It didn't matter if it wasn't as good as it ought to be; it could even be argued that it might intimidate people if it were. The ploy was to supply just enough truth to justify the show, but not so much as to jar anyone.

This, I supposed, was what they had. Unfortunately, however, they had jarred me in the process.

I reached for the phone and called Susskind at home. He sounded pleased to hear from me.

"I've thought it over, David," I said, "and I don't see how I can go along with you on this."

"What!"

"I'm sorry, but the answer is 'No deal.' "

Beat. Sound of deep breathing, a slight moan.

"I'm warning you, Eliot," and he cut loose with one final threat. "You'll regret this . . ."

When I made no reply, he hung up, leaving me like a craven drunk to issue my final denunciation into the dead phone.

"Up yours, David Susskind!"

A day later, Bill Storke called to report that he had just been apprised of my decision, and as a result, NBC was dropping the show. He made no comment. He did not even indicate any emotion one way or another, and I could not help wondering what he really felt about this whole mess—and especially about me; yet all I could do was thank him for his civilities, and that was the end of it.

And so the war ended, or at least this phase of it. From where I sat, I had won, though, whatever else it might be, I could hardly call it a victory. Nonetheless, I reveled in it, albeit quietly, feeling more as though something good would happen because of it than something bad.

Then, two months later, my ringing doorbell ended that magnificent silence. And when I saw the strange man in the plaid shirt—then the folded papers in his hand—I knew again how wrong I could be.

BOOK TWO

" *I wish I hadn't cried so much!*" said Alice, as she swam
about, trying to find her way out. "*I shall be punished for
it now, I suppose, by being drowned in my own tears!
That* will *be a queer thing, to be sure! However,
everything is queer today.*"

15.

As absurd as it sounds, I was now facing an ever-growing suspicion that *Eight Men Out* was actually cursed.

Just like those who had tampered with the tomb of Tutankhamen, anyone who came in contact with my book (most of all, me) would confront a lot of trouble.

Had not the book itself been conceived as a result of an abortion—when Ford Frick, commissioner of baseball in 1960, forced the cancellation of my television script?

Indeed, the resulting publicity had attracted the eye of a publisher named Howard Cady, then editor in chief at G. P. Putnam's Sons.

"Doesn't it strike you as absolutely incredible that no major work has ever been written about the Black Sox Scandal?" he asked me at lunch.

Unquestionably, this was an extremely fertile area for exploration. The impact of the Scandal had been striking, an opening wedge into the chilling amorality of the Roaring Twenties, the very roots of a growing cynicism leading many to believe that all major sporting events were fixed, that everything could be fixed, from traffic tickets to world wars. It was, then, an irresistible project, and I leaped at it, undeterred by the intensity of research that would have to be done, the unfolding of layer after layer of intrigue, the thousands of miles I would have to cover to find my sources.

"It'll take me at least a year," I said.

"Time is not a factor," he assured me.

Thus a book was conceived. I was to receive an advance of $2,500, half on signing the contract, the balance on delivery of an acceptable manuscript. It never crossed my mind that my expenses would run many times that figure merely to pursue the investigation. I simply did not care. I was a writer, not a businessman. This was going to be a labor of love. Besides, the way I saw it, $2,500 was merely an advance against royalties. The big money would come after publication.

As I write this now, it seems appalling that I should have accepted such a deal. Even in 1960, this was a pittance considering the grandiose scope of the venture. At the time, however, I held the process of authorship in awe, a creative experience to be treasured not exploited. I was still relatively untested, having published one baseball novel, *Man on Spikes*, five years before. Books about the sporting world, like sports movies, simply did not do well in 1960. To write about baseball again was to fly in the face of established norms, or so the argument went.

But then, I have always been foolish enough to disregard such arguments.

There were bad omens from the start. I had hardly banked that first $1,250 of my advance when I heard that James T. Farrell had recently completed a book about this exact same subject. Farrell, the great Chicagoan, distinguished author of *Studs Lonigan*, an old-time baseball fan who had followed the White Sox as a youth, was old enough to have actually experienced the 1919 World Series fix. How could I possibly compete with him?

Since he had favorably reviewed *Man on Spikes* a number of years before, I dared to call him. He immediately invited me to visit.

His apartment in the East Forties was memorable for its book-covered walls—huge stacks from floor to ceiling that, like any overburdened library, exuded a marvelous mustiness.

"Is it true that you've written a book about the Black Sox?" I asked him.

He nodded, and I felt a dead weight hit the pit of my stomach. "I had to know." I smiled bravely. "Better than spending a year or so writing a book you've already written . . ."

He looked at me through extremely heavy lenses, still sickly from a recent bout with the flu, his face gray-stubbled after days without shaving. "My book . . ." he began rather tentatively, "it doesn't seem to work. My publisher suggested I put it aside for a while." They were words spoken in distress, and they staggered me. The thought that a work about the Black Sox by such a giant as Farrell should not be worthy of publication was more than I could absorb at the moment.

"Has this ever happened to you before?" It seemed terribly impertinent to ask, but somehow I had to know. "I mean, with any other work?"

"No," he said. It was weird, for it seemed like a thought that had never occurred to him before. "It's not an easy book to write," he went on. "There's so much at stake and so little to go on . . ."

"So little?" I asked, not understanding.

"Yes. They won't talk. The ballplayers won't talk."

"How would you explain that?"

"That's for you to find out," he replied.

I was confused and more than a little intimidated. If James T. Farrell could not lick the Black Sox Scandal, how could I?

He saw my concern and smiled. "There's no reason for you not to go ahead, Eliot. In fact, you're the one to do it."

What's more, he immediately plunged into the material, quoting from his remarkable memory, jotting down notes as he spoke. "Nobody has really taken it on. Except for John Lardner's piece in the *Saturday Evening Post*, there's barely been a glimmer of truth written anywhere . . ."

He rattled off old salaries, batting averages, who was alive, how to get to them. He told me where there were likely to be blind alleys, suggested which newspapermen I should see, and others to see but not to trust.

Then he set the basic problem of the story in a few simple words. "Why did they do it?"

"You've got to get to those ballplayers, Eliot."

The way he felt, if I could answer that question of why, with depth and compassion, if I could relate it to the ethos of the times, if I could at least suggest an inevitability, "you'll not only have written a fine book, you'll have written a piece of history."

So it was that I went from foreboding to inspiration.

I began work the easy way, plunging into the New York libraries and newspaper files. After six such weeks, I'd read everything available, but I had no answers to basic questions. Just facts and background and other people's speculations—the stuff of a reasonably sound college term paper, but totally without substance.

I was ready to go for the real story. It would be like pulling a wolf's tooth.

Of the eight banished ballplayers from the 1919 White Sox, four were still alive. Over the next few months I would visit each of them, only to be rebuffed, one by one, as if their appalling silence were part of the conspiracy itself.

The one I most wanted to meet was the ace pitcher, Ed Cicotte. In August of 1919, when first baseman Chick Gandil began putting the nefarious scheme together, the first man he'd approached was Cicotte. Cicotte had been the Main Man on the White Sox staff, a veteran twenty-nine-game winner, an artful control pitcher who, at thirty-five, still had a sneaky fast ball. Cicotte would pitch the Series opener and as many games as his aging arm could cope with. It would be hard to fix the World Series without including him. Gandil figured it would be easy if he had him in the bag.

I had read reports of his tortured confession before a Cook County Grand Jury, how he had joined up with Gandil, insisting on $10,000 cash before the first game—which he found under his pillow in the Cincinnati Hotel Sinton, then immediately sewed into the lining of his coat. He had been bitter over Comiskey's broken promises—like the $10,000 bonus for winning thirty games, which was aborted by not letting him pitch on the very brink of it; or the meager salary Comiskey paid him over the years, never more than $6,000. "I needed the money to pay the mortgage on my farm," Cicotte had confessed, then turned one of the classic phrases of the Black Sox Scandal: "I did it for the wife and kids."

I pictured Cicotte as a complex man, far more sophisticated than his seven colleagues. He had been a friend of Ring Lardner's, for example. A jocular figure in the locker room, highly respected, well liked by his teammates.

Born in Detroit, when he left baseball he went to live on that newly acquired farm in southern Michigan. In his later years, he'd become a game warden. Now, at seventy-seven, he was retired, living quietly with his wife.

I wrote him a letter to introduce myself, thinking it less intrusive than a phone call, accompanying it with a copy of *Man on Spikes*, that he might read of my baseball experience and point of view. He returned the book and the letter, on which he had written: "Sorry. Thanks for rembering [*sic*] me. E. Cicotte."

Remembering him? I couldn't get him out of my mind. Was there some way I could get to him? What would Farrell do in my shoes?

"I'd go to Detroit and knock on his door," Jim said.

I was in Detroit by noon the following day, my attaché case full of note pads and a tape recorder. Cicotte's wife greeted me at the door, and I explained that I'd come from New York specifically to see her husband. He came to the door, my first look at a Black Sox. He was a short man, clean-shaven, gray but healthy-looking. He listened politely when I told him who I was and what I wanted to do, and a great sadness appeared to come over him. When I finished, he merely shook his head, apologized, then turned away, leaving me with his wife.

She, too, was polite, regretful for the trouble I had taken.

I asked her, "Do you think that if there was money involved—?"

She shook her head immediately. It was certainly not a question of money.

"He just won't" was her reply, and I left Detroit with an empty hand.

In Chicago, I began calling center fielder Oscar "Happy" Felsch at his home in Milwaukee. After the Scandal, he'd run a tavern in his old neighborhood. From his wife, I learned he was very ill. I asked if I might visit, explaining my purpose. No, she said quickly, I'd be wasting my time, Oscar would never talk to me. So I wrote him a letter, telling him something of my own baseball background, explaining how much I needed his help, eager for an hour or so with him. And when I didn't hear from him, I called again. And again Mrs. Felsch denied me.

Arnold "Chick" Gandil, still another of the living Black Sox, was the celebrated ringleader of the eight. Several years before, he had published a "confession" of his involvement in the 1919 affair in *Sports Illustrated*, but it was essentially a whitewash. I called him, anticipating only his hostility. Surprisingly, however, he consented to see me, and I visited him in Calistoga, his home in the Napa Valley above San Francisco.

He was a big man over seventy years old, still looking as tough as nails. He was also as shrewd as his reputation indicated, as interested in what I was up to as I was intrigued by him. There were no warm moments when talking to Gandil. We met in a tavern where we talked for a while, then in his car, or walking down the main street of Calistoga. He would not invite me to his home, presumably because he felt I might interpret his affluence as an indication of his corruption. (I was told he lived in a fine house on a valued piece of land.) I got him talking about his youth, how he ran away from home in Minnesota, hopped freights into the Southwest and Mexico, where he played some semipro ball, boxed, worked in the copper mines—a life curiously similar to that of his contemporary, Jack Dempsey. He enjoyed these macho memories of his toughness, choosing to interpret them as representative of a better time in America. "Baseball was a rough life until you hit the majors and the big cities. All of a sudden you're wearing suits and ties, expensive shoes. All them big hotels and riding on Pullmans. It was a big thing, a real big thing." Big-city baseball took the boy Gandil out of the country, but, to reverse the adage, it also took the country out of the boy. He had been quick to blend well among the sharp city types, notably one East Coast gambler named Joseph "Sport" Sullivan, through whom he had cultivated a sharp eye for an angle.

But when it came to talking about the 1919 World Series, Gandil had nothing to contribute. He referred to his article in *Sports Illustrated*, once again describing himself as more sinned against than sinning. In fact, he did not see where he had anything more to say to me, certainly not without being paid for it. I told him I was trying to set the whole story down as accurately as I could, that there were dozens of people to see all over the country, that if I had to pay everyone, I would be bankrupt long before I could put a word on paper.

"Too damn bad," he said. "You writers are always feeding on the ballplayers . . ."

"The way I figure it, Mr. Gandil, you already made your money on history. There ought to be better reasons for talking about it now."

He looked at me as if I'd come straight from Mars, and that was the end of my visit.

Well, I'd gone down swinging, anyway.

Which left me with the last of the living four, the shortstop, Charles "Swede" Risberg, two hundred miles north to Weed, a small crossroads town near the Oregon border.

Like Felsch, Risberg ran a tavern, a well-known hangout in those parts, his name conspicuously displayed like one who had been a local hero. His reputation during his playing days had been one of considerable bullishness; he once threatened Joe Jackson with brutal physical punishment if he dared to talk. And Risberg, Jackson had conceded, was very much "a hard guy." As I entered the tavern, I had his youthful picture in mind, an eager, handsome, boyish Nordic face. Forty-odd years later, he was recognizable at once, balding and gray, his pale face relatively free of creases. Approaching seventy, he did not seem tough at all, but I could not erase the memory of what I had read.

Would *he* talk to me?

It was early afternoon, but there was a handful of drinkers in action, working people in worn denims and work shirts and high, thick-soled shoes. They noted my arrival at the bar with curiosity, a stranger from the city. They even grew silent as I ordered a beer, if only to hear the sound of my voice.

I introduced myself to Risberg. He seemed pleasant enough, though uninterested, perhaps sensing there was nothing in it for him. I took the bull by at least one of its horns and told him I was a writer from New York working on a history of baseball. That's about as far as I got. His look was so cutting, so full of suspicion, I knew I had no chance with him.

"I don't know no history, mister," he said.

"You played on one of the greatest teams of all time," I argued.

"I don't remember them days. Talk to the others, maybe they remember."

"I already have," I said, watching his eyes for a sign of curiosity. Surely he'd want to know if they had talked—anything to get us started.

"Then you don't need to talk to me," he said, and he walked away, leaving me with my beer.

I hung around for a while, trying to break into other conversations, but no one encouraged me. Having driven a long way, I hated to leave without taking something with me. The problem was becoming an irritant. How long was I to pursue an investigation in the face of adversity? I sat in Risberg's tavern feeling the weight of my weariness. All of the four living Black Sox had refused to talk. I had gone 0 for 4—in baseball parlance, "the horsecollar."

I didn't see Swede Risberg again. He was there, but I didn't look at him, not wanting to give him the satisfaction, I suppose. I put a dollar on the counter to pay for the beers and left.

16.

Largely as a result of Jim Farrell, I was welcomed in Chicago, his references starting a chain reaction of contacts that took me from one source to another.

Whatever clips were available in various Chicago newspapers were made available to me in well-organized folders from the morgues. I found other papers and documents in the Chicago Historical Society. Old sports reporters like Irving Vaughn and Warren Brown let me see their files, sharing the fruits of whatever they could recall.

After my failure to get anything significant out of the four Black Sox, my research in secondary sources seemed all the more vital. In Chicago, there was enough on microfilm to break a man's back, rolling it through the machines for hours, day after day. I had a compulsion to see it all—everything that had been written—terrified that I might miss something.

Then I found Urban "Red" Faber's number in the Chicago phone book. He was friendly but wary, finally agreeing to meet me at his neighborhood Little League field, where his young son was playing.

Faber had been a great star with the White Sox, a remarkably durable pitcher who had one ailing year, 1919. There are many who said that the Sox would not have lost, fix or no fix, had Faber been working in that Series.

"It's tough to talk about it," he said. "I see some of the boys—like Schalk, for instance—and though he was as straight as an arrow, he won't even mention the Series. They were scared, I guess. Scared of the gamblers. Why, the hoodlums had some of the boys in their pocket all through the 1920 season too, throwing ball games right up to the last week of the pennant. I could feel it out there when I pitched—Risberg letting an easy ground ball go by, or Happy Felsch letting a runner take an extra base. You want to scream at them but you don't because you can see how scared they are."

Had Faber ever been approached to throw a game?

He laughed at my query. "No . . . I guess they can smell out a straight arrow pretty good. They didn't like me at all."

He was obviously proud of that, especially since ". . . it was a rotten time, all right. There was so much crookedness in those days, I guess we didn't pay too much attention to it. And that's pretty terrible. That's pretty damn terrible . . ."

I was touched by the poignancy of the comment, thinking how significant it was, a telling reaction to the climate of the times.

"Too bad you never got to see Buck Weaver," he said. Weaver, who died in 1956, was just about the best third baseman around. He never participated in the throwing of the games, or took a dime of any gambler's money, but was banished simply for his refusal to snitch on his friends. Weaver had never stopped trying to clear himself. He was so certain he could, for a while he even refused to play semipro ball with the others, thinking it might make it tougher for him to convince the commissioner.

"He really got a bad deal," Faber went on. "He was straight all the way. The way he loved to play ball, it was his whole life. The guy would no more throw a ball game than murder his wife. When he got too old to play, he wanted to coach, but even then they wouldn't let him, and that really busted him up. He carried that around with him till he died."

"You really liked him," I offered.

"Everybody in baseball liked him. Chicago fans loved him. This used to be some baseball town . . ." Then he shook his head ruefully. "The poor guy dropped dead of a heart attack, right in the street. He was young. And he wasn't the only one. Kid Gleason (manager of the Sox) was ruined by the Scandal. I remember, after that first game in Cincy when they whipped Cicotte, Gleason went nuts. He knew what was going on. Most everybody did. He started yelling at Cicotte and Swede Risberg in the hotel lobby in front of a hundred people, he didn't give a damn who heard him. Can you imagine a manager doing that? He died of a heart attack too. I heard that Joe Jackson had three heart attacks. I really believe the Scandal did it."

If Faber was cooperative and friendly, Ray Schalk was quite the opposite. I called him at Purdue University, where he was coaching baseball, asking if I might see him for an interview.

"What about?" he asked.

"You're a famous man in the baseball world, Mr. Schalk," I said, staying clear of the Scandal at the moment.

"I don't cotton much to writers."

"Well, I'm an old ballplayer too," I noted.

"You're a writer now," he said.

For all his wariness, he was polite, and I told him I'd be in Lafayette the following morning if he had a free hour.

"Come along, if it's that important," he said.

It was. It definitely was.

He was solid granite. The first mention of the Black Sox turned him off. At first I thought this might be his sour mood, the result of yesterday's defeat of his ball club or an argument with his wife, but I was wrong.

"Like I said, mister, you're wasting your time and mine."

"Mr. Schalk, you're a hero to me. You represent resistance to corruption. What you had to do in that Series . . ."

". . . Mister, I'm not talking about it," he snapped.

"May I ask why?"

"Forget it," he said, turning to papers on his desk.

"You dislike *all* writers?" I asked.

He refused to answer, mumbling something as he turned away, obviously wanting to be done with this. I had to get at the source of his resentments, even if it meant provoking him.

"Why, Mr. Schalk? That seems like such a paranoid view. Like a black kid in the ghetto when he faces a cop—*any* cop."

He looked back at me, eyes flaring, saying nothing, for what seemed like a long time, no doubt trying to control his temper.

"What do you know what I think?" he said. "I'll tell you something: No, I don't trust writers. I've seen too many of them, they don't get as close to an umpire as to a bartender. They know nothing about baseball. They hang around picking up stories they got no right to hear, always making everything come out worse than it was. They're a bunch of old-lady gossips. What do I want to talk to you for?"

For all his hostility, I was struck by the honesty of his emotion. Obviously he had thought much about this over the years. I could picture his intensity during his playing career when sportswriters did nothing to expose the ongoing corruption until it was too late, many of them flacks who wrote out of Charles Comiskey's pocket. How many distortions and inanities would have to appear in the papers before a hard-nosed straight shooter like Schalk would become repelled by all sportswriting? I could imagine him telling a story to some eager young reporter only to see it read differently because "my boss wouldn't let me run it the way you told it to me."

Even in my own limited experience in the minor leagues, I was aware of this sort of game playing. The small-town writers I'd met were a mixed bag of old rummies and young hacks, whose persistently idiotic questions reflected their ignorance. We were kids, most of us, eager and polite and cooperative, loving baseball, struggling for the next notch up the minor-league ladder. Some of the more guileful of us learned how to use sportswriters the way a wily child learns how to use a schoolteacher, but what appeared in the papers was usually an embarrassment. Once I went on a lucky hitting streak—a lot of handle hits, pop flies that dropped in, squibbles through the infield. I went something like 14 for 26, hardly making solid contact. The sportswriters, responding to my .429 batting average, began building me up as a real slugger. The way they saw it, the statistics were the thing. But in the sanctity of the team bus, I was the butt of daily jokes about broken bats and bloody hands. Every ballplayer knows the difference between a real hitter and a lucky one.

And years before that, when I was a twelve-year-old Yankee fan, Lou Gehrig had gone something like 2 for 29, and the writers were pouring on daily articles about how Gehrig was in a terrible hitting slump. I went up to the stadium that Sunday for the doubleheader during which Gehrig drilled six line drives of enormous power, all of them caught, some at impressive distances. The next day's papers had it that Gehrig's slump continued, his timing was off, he needed a rest. No writer noticed that all of those vicious drives were on Gehrig's *first swing;* he wasn't fouling off several or missing swings or taking strikes; he was really hitting sensationally well!

And now I was getting thrown out of Ray Schalk's office. He was a tiger, all right, and the more I came to know about him from others, the more it fed the image. I could picture him behind the plate, raging at those cream puffs Ed Cicotte was throwing to him in that first Series game, shouting through those iron bars until his throat rasped in pain. Then, after the second game, another loss manipulated by Lefty Williams, Schalk exploded, waited for Williams under the grandstand, and vented his fury with his fists. Schalk never said a word about that fight, certainly not to any writer, and when the story leaked, his rage was equally great against its exposure. The eventual betrayal of the Series by his teammates became a blot on him as well. He could not bear the shame of the fix, for this was his team, these were the men he lived with, this was the game he played and loved.

Years after my book was published, Ray Schalk, then over seventy, sat on the dais as guest of honor at the annual Baseball Writers Association banquet in New York. At the bar with Joe DiMaggio before the dinner, I told the story of my meeting with Schalk, wondering if he might have mellowed.

"Let's find out," DiMag suggested, volunteering to lead me to him.

"Ray, you remember Eliot Asinof?" DiMag offered. "He wrote that fine book on the Black Sox?"

Schalk barely looked up, and though I was standing behind him, I could see his body tense.

"I don't want him near me!" he snapped.

Schalk died in 1970, without ever saying a bloody word.

The third-ranking pitcher on the 1919 White Sox (not one of the eight men out) was a remarkable little left-hander named Dickie Kerr, who succeeded in winning two games in that Series with half of his own team working to lose it. I caught up with him in Houston, where Commissioner Ford Frick awarded him a silver tray in a special ceremony in his honor.

Kerr was a retiree in his late sixties, his slight body, seemingly diminished by age, looking more like an old railroad engineer than an ex–major leaguer. Like Faber, he was not averse to talking.

I asked him if he had known he was working against super odds when he pitched those two games.

"Oh, I'd heard things, sure. Everybody heard things. But, you know, you walk on that hill, you don't think about anything but throwing it by the hitter."

"Could you see anything about the way Cicotte and Williams were working? Could you tell they were letting up?"

He shook his head sadly, unable to answer. "All those guys, they didn't know what they were doing."

His baseball career was far too short for a man of his talents. And that, too, resulted from the World Series fix.

"It was a sad thing to see that club fall apart. One year the best, then in 1921, seventh—what were we, thirty-seven games behind the Yankees? That's a tough go when you're used to playing for a winner."

I reminded him that he himself had always been a winner, even in 1921. He nodded with a modest smile. "Comiskey didn't seem to care," he said. "Least not when it came to contract time."

Dickie Kerr had won the right to a substantial raise, but was offered infinitely less. "I just couldn't sign for sixty-five hundred. I refused to believe Comiskey wouldn't raise me. It became like a regular war, both of us standing firm. I s'pose he felt it would be bad to give in, then others would hold out and he'd lose his power. What broke me was at training camp, Mr. Comiskey's son Lou was in charge. I hadn't signed. I wanted to discuss it, but he snubbed me. He wouldn't even talk to me. So I just packed my gear and left."

Following so closely on the heels of the Scandal itself, this treatment of Kerr loomed as the ultimate of Comiskey's folly. The trouble was that if Kerr did not agree to terms, he could not play organized professional baseball anywhere. It was an added irony that

Kerr ended up playing semipro ball with his old banished teammates. And to top it all, when Kerr chose to return to Chicago, Commissioner Landis chose to punish him for that, forcing him to serve a year's penance.

As it ended up, Comiskey and Landis dumped him into the same pot with the eight Black Sox. "Loyal, disloyal, you were all treated the same," I offered.

"And now the commissioner of baseball gives me a trophy . . ." he said.

The Black Sox tragedy had come full circle with Dickie Kerr.

Though "Shoeless" Joe Jackson had been dead for a decade, I visited his home in Brandon Mill, South Carolina, a small cotton-mill town outside of Greenville that showed few signs of change since he grew up there. I walked down the abbreviated main drag with its small, drab shops, visited the mill where Joe had worked twelve hours a day as a boy (along with his father, six brothers, and two sisters). I found one of his sisters with a marvelous scrapbook, and more than a few others with vivid memories. Totally illiterate, Joe had nonetheless bought a home for his parents, set up businesses for himself. One, a pool parlor in Greenville, another, a large farm nearby. He became a slick dresser by hometown standards, loving the feel of shiny new shoes and a flashy hat. Everyone seemed to think fondly of him.

"He never got over the Scandal thing," his sister said. "He went into the valet business [dry cleaning], then opened a liquor store. He did fine. He kept playing semipro ball around Greenville, and even though he put on some weight, at forty-four he was still the darndest hitter you ever saw."

In his later years, Jackson apparently began to reappraise his guilt, even succeeded in convincing himself that he had done no wrong, falling back on the fact that they'd all been acquitted at the trial. In 1949, *Sport* magazine ran his story, a concoction of depressing distortions. The way I read it, it summed up all the confusions of a life he could never understand. The world of baseball was too much for any of them, and especially a primitive like Jackson. They had lived in a jungle without moral leadership. A pompous man like Charles Comiskey (he was called "The Old Roman") had had nothing to do with them off the field. They lived on the fringes of American society, classless, exploited, extolled by fans. Unlike coal miners, perhaps, or farmers, they had no semblance of stability. All they had was each other. They drank a lot, played cards, sat around hotel lobbies waiting for those daily afternoons on the ball field, literally wasting the rest of the day. Inevitably, they would become bored with each other and themselves. The only class of people who understood them were the gamblers. Seductive operators with flashy styles, sharp men who knew the best places in town, they would offer the visiting players something to do, bathe them in flattery, speak the right language, always with a full measure of respect. All this for a price, and in 1919, a very dear one.

Placing all this in the larger setting that was America after the horrors of World War I, a reversion to the moral vacuousness of "normalcy," it is not difficult to understand what drove primitives like Jackson into trouble—and the ease with which they might subsequently rationalize their denial of it.

There is a poignant story of Ty Cobb shopping at Jackson's liquor store. While Cobb bought a quart of Bourbon, neither indicated the slightest sign of recognition.

Finally, Cobb spoke up. "What's the matter, Joe . . . don't you know me?"

"Sure, I know you, Ty. I just didn't think anyone I used to know up there wanted to recognize me again."

Of Jackson's last years, his sister talked of a belated attempt to clear his name. In 1951, he was asked to come to New York to appear on the "Ed Sullivan Show," but a few weeks before his scheduled appearance, he suffered a third heart attack and died.

"Everybody liked Joe," his sister said. "It was the biggest funeral that Greenville ever saw."

17.

I returned to New York and took stock of what I'd accomplished.

Not very much, as it turned out.

I'd covered over ten thousand miles of hard travel for perhaps seventy-five pages of manuscript.

I had some fine background material, but no real insights.

I knew everything that had been written about the Scandal, but it added up to very little.

I went over my notes carefully, then organized the material as if I were preparing to construct the book. The best I could arrange was a skimpy outline with far more holes than substance.

It was enormously depressing.

I began speculating that perhaps it couldn't be done, it was a piece of history too elusive for historians. It had licked James T. Farrell, hadn't it? On one of my lesser days, I even called Howard Cady at G. P. Putnam's Sons to discuss my problems, presumably with an eye to quitting the project. I was told, however, that Cady was no longer there, having recently shifted to the head editor's job at Holt, Rinehart and Winston.

This left me in limbo, which was exactly where I'd been when I called. Curiously, the resulting confusion was something of a comfort, for it seemed to justify the way I was leaning. If publishers could be unreliable, why not depressed writers?

I didn't call Cady at his new offices, nor did I bother to learn who would replace him at Putnam's.

For several weeks I simply did nothing about it, neither working nor planning to work. I thought of calling Jim Farrell but decided against it: I didn't care to confess my defeat to him. Not yet, at any rate. Nor was I in the mood for any attempt to inspire me.

I simply sulked.

However, it must be noted that this was spring, and, as was my habit, I played softball in Central Park in the Broadway Show League, a weekly game of sufficient quality and competitiveness to set it a few rungs above what its name might imply. I had long since joined forces with a team representing the Circle in the Square, a Greenwich Village establishment at the time, whose artistic director, Ted Mann, also ran the ball club. On this particular Thursday afternoon we were pitted against the highly rated team from CBS, whose pitcher was Jim Jensen, and whose shortstop was Phil Rizzuto.

Over twenty-five years before, I had played ball against Rizzuto in a strong weekend league out on Long Island known as the Queens Alliance. I had been a high school hotshot at the time, with the beginnings of a reputation around the area. One Sunday afternoon in Rockaway, I was told that Paul Kritchell, the famous Yankee scout, was in the stands to watch me play. Fired up, I hit two doubles—one on either side of the center fielder—beat out a cagey bunt, stole a base, and went proudly to the bench at the game's end to wait for Kritchell's offer. When I looked up, however, he was sitting on the opposite bench talking to that tiny kid who played shortstop.

The rest is history, as they say, for Rizzuto played a dozen great seasons in the majors. On this afternoon in Central Park, since I had not confronted him in all the intermittent years, I had no reason to think he'd remember me. I did not bother to say hello. We were there to play a ball game, not to socialize.

When I came to bat, however, I saw that I was wrong about his memory. I had no sooner set up in the batter's box, made one or two preliminary moves with the bat, when I saw him staring at me from behind the pitcher.

"Hold it," he called to Jensen, then turned to the outfielders (who had shifted toward right) and moved them back to a straight-away position. He himself edged two or three steps toward third to cover the hole.

It was so incredible, I stepped out laughing. After twenty-five years, he had actually recognized me by my batting stance, remembering where I liked to hit. He saw me laughing and laughed himself, obviously pleased at his own capacities.

"Queens Alliance!" he called out.

I nodded, and waved a greeting.

"Play ball!" the umpire barked.

It was a marvelous moment, and it carried me through the day, another reminder of what baseball had meant to me. Though well over forty, Rizzuto could still move like a scooter and had been a treat to watch.

"You still take a fine cut at it," he said to me.

"A man can hit until he goes blind," I noted.

The following morning, I went to my desk for the first time in weeks. I reread what I had and saw what I had to do. I'd had my moments of despair. It was now time to see about filling all those holes in the story.

I called Abe Attell, "The Little Champ," as he was called, the insidious manipulator and Artful Dodger of the fix, the old fighter and consort of Arnold Rothstein.

It was no small relief to note that he was happy to hear from me.

I was determined to go to the canvas with Attell. Months before, we had talked, and in my ignorance, I had been taken in by his garbled account, another self-serving confession of innocence in exchange for $500 from *Cavalier* magazine. If "The Little Champ" was not an out-and-out liar, he had reached that point of self-deception wherein history became warped by his need to purify his image.

"Champ, last time we talked, you said it was Arnold Rothstein who fixed the Series. You said you had nothing to do with it except to make a few bets and tip a few friends. Now I have all these notes telling me how *you* sat in meetings with the ballplayers, how it was *you* who were the driving force behind the fix, how *you* promised them scads of money, which you did not deliver . . ."

He never batted an eye. "Well, I tell you, pally, I may have gotten a few things mixed up." Then he jabbed a playful fist into my ribs. (I could now tell everyone that I'd taken a punch from Abe

Attell!) He was an amazing character, a master at leaning on the friendliness of those he wished to use. I could picture him in the years before the Scandal, a tiny, dazzling, dapper young champion, darting in and out of prestigious saloons where the powerful politicians and sporting crowd gathered, an ambitious young operator looking to get into the action. ("We would hang around the old Metropole Hotel in Times Square, owned by George Considine and Big Tim Sullivan, the Tammany boss of New York. . . . It was the scene of some mighty big crap games and poker games, big drinking parties, big political wheeling and dealing, and even a big murder. It was there the gambler Herman Rosenthal was murdered in that famous case involving Police Captain Charles Becker.") It was where Attell had latched on to Arnold Rothstein, one of the biggest operators of all.

As for the start of the World Series fix, I threw the hard evidence back at him. "When the gamblers first came to A.R. at the racetrack, he was too busy to talk to them. He sent them to the track restaurant to wait, then told you to go see what they wanted. They told you that they had eight ballplayers in the bag, ready to throw the Series. All they needed was a hundred thousand dollars to finance it. You went back to A.R. and reported this, but he said no, he didn't want a part of it. But you saw a way to use his name and do it yourself. Champ, you pulled off a whopper, didn't you. You went back to the restaurant and told those gamblers that A.R. said yes, he *would* back them! Now, isn't that the way it happened?"

Again, that sly, impish grin, its roots in the art of manipulation, the more devious the better.

"Well now, pally, I couldn't throw away a chance like that, could I? I mean, it was a once-in-a-lifetime shot!"

His boldness had been fabulous. He would defy and betray a man as powerful as Arnold Rothstein—who was absolutely certain to learn of the ploy—and never even speculate on the consequences. I thought of the ballplayers, innocents one and all (with the exception of Chick Gandil), who remained terrified for the remainder of their lives.

"So *you* were the key man, Champ."

He was more than that. He was a snake who crawled through those Cincinnati-to-Chicago hotel rooms and lobbies and Pullman cars, fertilizing the deceit-ridden drama with his insidious droppings.

"It was a game of cheaters cheating cheaters, pally," he said. "A man has to make a dollar, you know."

One could imagine the tribulations of the newly retired champion trying to make a living in those days. He had tried the vaudeville circuit, demeaning himself with a phony song-and-dance act, telling gag-written stories about his experiences in the fight game. He was not the type to sell insurance or work for a hard-earned dollar. Abe slid easily into the gray areas of "legitimate" corruption, and subsequently into anything at all.

I worked hard on him, and even harder on myself. I surrounded myself with the period, reading nothing but historical material. Baseball history was only a part of it. I wanted to know the kind of cars they were driving, the movies they saw, the papers and magazines they read. By an extraordinary coincidence, the neighborhood in which I lived became helpful. On Seventy-third Street and Broadway, the Ansonia Hotel was only a block from my apartment, a landmark not only in the city's history, but in the baseball world of 1919. In its halls Hal Chase had walked, and the White Sox hung out there when they were in New York. Across the street was the site of the famous old Reuben's Restaurant. Arnold Rothstein lived ten blocks away, just off Riverside Drive, in a town house that was still standing. At the time of the Scandal, his father, a highly respected man called "Abe the Just," lived on West Seventy-first Street, in the very house I grew up in. And down the block was the Alamac Hotel, where Babe Ruth stayed. How many Saturday mornings had I stood as a boy under its marquis, waiting for him to appear en route to Yankee Stadium. He would emerge like a giant, smiling, always smiling, and the other kids would rush up to him with their pens and autograph books. He'd sign them all, talking to them all, and then once he noticed me, he really noticed me, and walked over.

"Hey kid, how come you don't want an autograph too?"

I shrugged, too overawed to answer. Then he laid his hand on my head and affectionately messed up my hair. I went home beaming, refusing to comb my hair for days.

By 1960, this sporting social center had long since moved downtown, and Attell and I moved among such popular haunts as Gallagher's Steak House on Fifty-second Street, and Jack Dempsey's Restaurant, a few blocks south on Broadway. He would love to be seen there at the peak lunch hours or cocktail time, and he would proudly introduce me to everyone he knew as "The Writer."

" 'The Writer' is writing a book about me," he'd say. Not about the Black Sox Scandal, but about Abe Attell. Nor was this a willful distortion of my intent, it was simply the way he saw it. He was flattered that anyone would care to spend that much time probing into his memories—easy enough to understand, for he had little else to do.

One afternoon, Abe was telling me stories at Dempsey's, enjoying the presence of a half-dozen others (including Dempsey himself), reveling in the way his words kept my pen moving across my note pad. This time, however, he was exceeding himself in Attellian hogwash, and I simply stopped writing.

"What's a matter, pally, you tired or something?" he asked.

"I'm tired of nonsense, Champ," I said.

He started to protest, then rose to his five feet, three inches.

"I gotta go piss," he said.

Dempsey sat looking at me, his large, friendly face forming the beginning of a rueful smile. I smiled back, more curious than amused.

"What . . . ?" I asked him.

He gestured toward my pen and note pad, shaking his head. "I'd rather fight Tunney for nothing than have to do that."

In the end, I managed to force Attell into a position where he had to tell the truth. He would admit his deceptions but furiously defend his right to deceive. Yes, he had lied to the gambler Bill Burns at the racetrack. Then he had lied to A.R. And he subsequently lied to the eight Black Sox, after which he cheated them out of the money that was due them. That he had also tipped off a few of his distinguished friends (like the great showman George M. Cohan) was just another stratagem to ingratiate himself. He didn't want to take advantage of *everybody*. To me, he became a gold mine of information, all of which was delivered in barely decipherable jargon. Or, as my tape recorder would reveal Attell on the exposure of the Scandal:

"It was Cicotte begun the blow job [confessed] to the Grand Jury. I was in New York at the time, and believe me, A.R. was doing the shakes [frightened] too. So we have this meeting at his place on Riverside Drive and the Big Mouthpiece is there, [William J.] Fallon, doncha know, and Sport Sullivan from Boston. And Fallon says to us: 'There's so much jabber in the rags [newspapers] about the dirty cereal [World Series], maybe this McCoyle [Maclay Hoyne, Cook County D.A.] is gonna extradite and I don't wanna see A.R. or you guys go to Chicago, I wanna see you guys skip town, alla you, as far as you can go.' And A.R. says: 'Here's a coupla bills to keep you loose. Champ, you go to Canada and cover yourself up, and Sully go to Mexico. Me, I'm going all the way to Europe.' So I grab the first train to Montreal like he says and like I know I'm a sucker to go 'cause A.R. is a worm of the top floor, even his best pals say he's so slimy he gives worms a bad rep, doncha know. So when I read in the rags up in Montreal that he didn't go to Europe at all, he crawled to Chicago with the Mouthpiece and squealed to the Grand Jury that he had nothing to do with the fix, he even told 'em that he didn't even bet on it, that it was *me* who put the cereal in the bag . . ."

For all his deceits and obfuscations, the pieces finally came together. I even got the feeling that he was genuinely trying to help me in his fashion. His enthusiasm never waned, nor did he complain when it must have become apparent that my appraisal of his role in the Scandal was highly uncomplimentary. His pride and his pleasure were satisfied with his own oft-repeated dictum: "Without me, pally, you wouldn't have a book."

I did not dissuade him of this slant, though a more accurate impression might be: "Without you, Champ, we wouldn't have had the Scandal."

Knowing him in his last years, I regretted never having seen him fight, picturing the wily, smart-ass pluckiness that must have doubled his fighting skills. Three hundred and sixty-five professional bouts. Beaten only six times. Never knocked out. Attell was so good, there were boxing experts who claimed that he never lost except when he wanted to.

"Did you ever take a dive, Champ?" I once asked him.

"Aw, come on, pally."

"I've heard responsible people who said you did."

Indeed, the record has it that he was suspended in 1912 after an exceptionally shaky fight.

"Well, a coupla times I held bums up for a few extra rounds . . ."

He was seventy-two years old, but he never quit. In the midst of the long months I was working on the book, he called me one night from Miami (collect), desperate that I wire him $200 immediately.

"You in trouble, Champ? What happened?"

"No, no trouble, pally. I just got to get some extra money down for the fight."

A fix, I thought immediately. My God, was the Dykes-Fullmer fight in the bag? Maybe Abe even had something to do with the fixing, and there was a chance for me to cash in on the kind of inside poop that enabled "smart" people to drive Cadillacs.

"Who's going to win, Champ?"

"Two C notes, pally. I'm staying at the Fontainebleau."

"Abe, *who*???"

"No questions. Just wire the dough!"

Then he hung up. He simply didn't have time for discussions. I could picture this same man in 1919, that same frantic voice calling anyone and everyone to borrow money to get down as much as he could on Cincinnati.

I had to laugh. It was like being part of a historical rerun.

As I worked, the sounds of his amorality kept ringing in my ears, his deviousness the guiding ethic of my writing. In a way, then, it *was* a book about him, the more painful since it represented one great athlete betraying others. How much simpler it would have been for me if Attell were merely a pimp or a slimy racetrack tout. Or even if he had somehow gotten the best of a big-time gambler like Rothstein, who, in the course of things, had flicked him off his sleeve like a pesky bug. What a pair they must have been, "The Little Champ" and "The Big Bankroll." Whatever the discrepancies in power and wealth and savvy, they were merely two rats fighting in rancid hallways for the cheese. If Attell had set the fix in motion, it was never out of my speculations that Rothstein might have stopped it, that a man as big as he might somehow respect the game enough to prevent its evisceration. Weren't gangsters and gamblers supposed to be patriotic Americans? It was a mark of Rothstein's character that he should choose to feed off it (he won over $350,000 betting on the Cincinnati Reds, most of it from the oil tycoon, Harry F. Sinclair), then extend the corruption by manipulating the cover-up, abetted by that glamorous member of the bar, William J. Fallon. Fallon, indeed. How he made a mockery of the law with his preposterous tactics, subverting the system with bribes and threats and illicit deals in the tragicomic opera that followed the Series! That Comiskey himself should end up in bed with A.R., collaborators in the denouement, was a supercynical poet's dream.

"Cheaters cheating cheaters," Attell had called it, but his was the penny-ante variety in contrast to the way the real power worked for profits and self-preservation.

No wonder Ford Frick had been wary of a television special.

18.

Weeks later, back in Chicago again, I would learn the art and depth of the real corruption.

I went probing in the basement of the Cook County Courthouse for whatever records might be available, only to be laughed at by the clerk. History had recorded that the Grand Jury testimony had been stolen back in 1921. Even the transcript of the Black Sox trial no longer existed.

"There's nothing here?" I asked.

"Dozens of guys have already looked, mister."

Up in the main lobby, I dallied aimlessly, lost among speculations as to where I might probe for I knew not what, eventually finding myself in front of a glass-enclosed call-board announcing trials in progress, and one judge's name caught my eye: Friend. (Exactly what I needed, one might say.)

The name stuck in my mind for a variety of reasons, not the least of which was a recollection that, at the trial of the Black Sox in 1921, the presiding judge was named Friend. A memorable name, to be sure. Indeed, had it been Smith or Brown, either then or here and now, I would have given it no further thought.

But Friend?

Could there be a connection?

It was a grope in the dark, for I didn't even know this judge's first name (nor, at the moment, could I recall that of the Black Sox judge). And since the 1921 trial was forty years earlier, it seemed highly unlikely that any Friend might be the same man.

Still . . .

I turned to the man standing beside me, attaché case in hand, obviously a young attorney.

"Counselor," I said, "what's Judge Friend's first name?"

"Hugo," he replied.

That rang the bell. That was it. Hugo Friend.

"How old is he?" I asked.

"Haven't the slightest idea," he said.

Immediately, I crossed the lobby to a phone, working my way through the switchboard to the judge's chambers, waiting anxiously for the telltale sound of his voice in hopes of it rasping with age.

"Yes . . . ?" He finally came on, and that single little word was enough.

He was old, all right.

I introduced myself, revealing the circumstances of my call, and he laughed, a marvelous outburst of joy and enthusiasm. "My goodness, I've been waiting forty years for someone to ask me about that case!"

I visited him the following afternoon. He was eighty-one years old, but as quick and alive as a man half his age. That no one had gotten to him before me only served to add zest to his revelations.

"I'll never forget it," he said. "It was my first major trial. By George, I was no older than the ballplayers!"

He described the political maneuvering that preceded the trial, what he considered to be a serious effort by the professional baseball world to keep it shelved. "They were making a farce out of the law. Those stolen confessions, for example . . . that was arranged by Arnold Rothstein's lawyer, William Fallon, but the man who gained the most from it was Comiskey himself."

"Do you think Comiskey was in on it?"

"Of course! I'd heard that Rothstein and Fallon met with Alfred Austrian, Comiskey's attorney, big Chicago law firm, you know. Without the confessions, the D.A. had no real case. In fact, the whole cover-up smacked of conspiracy," he went on. "Who, for example, paid for the ballplayers' lawyers? Why, they were the top criminal lawyers in the state. It cost more to set up that defense than the ballplayers made in a year!"

He explained that a deal might have been made: Rothstein's name would be kept out of the case. Abe Attell would not be extradicted. The ballplayers would be acquitted. Comiskey would have his great team intact, his million-dollar investment protected. Everyone would be happy.

"After the verdict, there was bedlam in the court." He smiled at his memory of it. "The jurors and the ballplayers actually embraced, the crowd cheered; it was something to see, all right. Why, they carried the ballplayers out on their shoulders. In forty years, I never saw anything like *that* again."

It was the cover-up that fascinated me. The thought of A.R. meeting with Comiskey made my head spin, high-powered lawyers like Fallon and Austrian plotting to circumvent the law. Could it really have happened that way? Was "The Old Roman" actually party to the theft of the Grand Jury testimony?

"There was a lawsuit up in Milwaukee a few years after," the judge recalled, "and the confessions turned up." He suggested I

111

check that out, even gave me the name of a clerk who might help me find the records.

The case in question involved Joe Jackson's suit against Comiskey for $18,000 back pay, his claim being that Comiskey had violated a three-year contract by refusing to pay Jackson after the suspension.

The record shows the following exchange, loosely paraphrased for brevity:

Defending Comiskey, attorney George B. Hudnall (a member of Alfred Austrian's firm) claimed it was Jackson who had failed to comply with his contract, not Comiskey. Had not Jackson sold out the World Series?

Raymond Cannon, Jackson's lawyer, immediately snapped: "The law has tried my client and acquitted him. Where, then, is there any proof that he had done that?"

Hudnall replied that Jackson had confessed.

"What confession?" Cannon demanded.

Whereupon Hudnall opened his briefcase and brought out the *original copy of Jackson's signed confession!*

"What!" Cannon roared. "How is it that these 'stolen' Grand Jury records are in *your* hands?"

Hudnall paled, turned toward Comiskey, and exchanged glances with him. "I don't know," said Comiskey.

"You don't know?" Cannon challenged him.

Comiskey, visibly ruffled, could only repeat, "I'm sorry, I don't know."

I could picture Jackson's amusement, bewildering though it must have been—the illiterate, primitive rube getting another taste of how the big-city magnate plays the game. In the end, Jackson won only a small part of the money due him, but for me, it had been a glorious discovery, and I laughed all the way to a nearby tavern.

On that afternoon, the beer tasted especially fine in Milwaukee. I sat on a barstool counting my blessings, one of those marvelous moments when all the effort seemed justified. I was going to be all right with this book, by God. This was what it was to be a journalist!

Two beers later, I was talking to the bartender about the Black Sox Scandal. He was too young to know much about it, but another barfly, a man of fifty or more, mentioned that he used to drink beer in Happy Felsch's tavern. "Real good guy," the man said. "Everybody liked him. Always used to tell crazy riddles, like 'How do porcupines screw?' Then he'd answer 'Very, very carefully.' Or he'd say, 'When wine, women, and song get to be too much for you, give up singing.' "

I was transfixed, clinging to every word he was saying as if I were gaining some marvelous new intimacy with Happy Felsch himself. I could actually picture him standing behind the bar telling jokes, and maybe nobody would laugh—they'd all heard them before—and I tried to imagine what Felsch would do.

Whatever, I suddenly knew I had to visit him. I'd get a cab and go to his house, ring the doorbell. Then I remembered a news story from 1920 wherein a reporter named Harry Reitlinger actually got Felsch to talk simply by visiting him with a bottle of Scotch.

Fifteen minutes later, I was standing in front of Felsch's house with a fifth of Chivas Regal in hand and an eager smile on my face. I was lucky, just as I knew I would be. Mrs. Felsch was weary of playing nursemaid to her sick husband, and this polite young visitor offered a welcome relief. She remembered my calls, the letter I'd written. She would let her husband deal with that. She took my coat, led me up a creaky old staircase and into a small, dark sitting room.

"Be kind to him," she said to me.

The television was on, an early-afternoon game show, but Felsch was asleep in a large chair, his heavily bandaged foot propped on the ottoman. She turned off the set, and the sudden silence awakened him.

"Oscar, you have a visitor."

I smiled in greeting, offered my hand as I spoke my name.

"How do porcupines screw?" I asked.

He was seventy years old and dying of cancer, but his ruddy-red complexion glowed when he smiled.

"Very, very carefully," he said.

"I need your help, Mr. Felsch," I said as I worked the bottle open. "I can't drink all this Scotch myself."

"Don't seem like too much to me," he replied.

Mrs. Felsch brought two tumblers, then left us to enjoy each other.

"You must've put the whammy on her," he said, but I could tell he was pleased.

And so it was that we talked for several hours, well down that bottle. He told me about himself. He had come from a German socialist background, his father was a strict authoritarian figure. "Hell, he had to be; there were twelve kids around the table. Can you imagine the babble if he'd allowed us to speak?" They were poor. Happy had to quit school after the sixth grade to take a factory job paying $10 a week—which he immediately handed to his father, who gave him back a quarter for his needs. "Being poor was nothing in those days. Everyone I knew was poor." Poverty was a fact of life, like the weather, and you found ways to enjoy yourself within its limitations. To Happy, the primary joy was playing ball, the only game in town. He was good, but so were hundreds of kids in Milwaukee. "Then, one winter—I was maybe fifteen—I shot up. Big, you know. That first day in spring, I hit one over the fence. None of us kids had ever done that, and the way they all looked at me, it was something, all right."

I knew the feeling. You grow up playing around a certain ball field, you watch grown men clear the outfield wall, and you wonder when you'll be big enough to do it. The Rite of Passage. It's the shot that can change your life.

Felsch was laughing at his memory. "Half the deal was to hit the long ones when the ball was still whole. Hell, we played with one baseball so long, you could hear it whimper when you hit it. After a while, it was hardly a baseball no more. Cover all gone, we'd tape it up. It wouldn't go nowhere. If you hit it, it'd make a strange sound, like a sharp fart, you know? And the pitcher had so many things to grab hold of, he could really make it dance. 'Course, most of the bats were no better. Nailed, glued up, taped . . . when a new bat broke, everyone'd look up, you know, and the sound'd make you sad." He laughed again. "Seems like all I ever wanted was to hit a new ball with a new bat."

He was a marvelous storyteller, humble without being self-deprecating, always amusing, as though he never really took life that seriously. His memory of New York, for example, consisted of a bus ride to Brooklyn wherein it took two hours to cross the Bowery, because kids were shooting craps in the streets, laughing at the bus driver, who couldn't get them to move no matter how much he honked his horn. Then, too, he had a few choice hates—Charles Comiskey was one, a man of such cheapness, "he made us feel like dogs." Nor did he like sportswriters. "All company men. You could bet they'd write what the old man wanted. The player didn't have a chance. No matter what was happening, if he felt Comiskey wouldn't like the story, he wouldn't write a word . . ." Then, pensively, "I may be dumb, but most o' them writers don't know half what I know." Then, twinkling, "Writers can't hit a baseball. If they could, they wouldn't be writers."

I told him I'd played some pro ball, and that sometimes I thought I could hit better than I could write. He laughed and asked me about my experiences, nodding his head when I told him how much I loved the game.

"For me, it was the way to get out of the factory," he said. "But I guess I'd've played ball even if it kept me working in there."

The game, that was the thing. "In a ball game, nothing else matters. Now, ain't that something! You wonder, am I gonna hit that guy's stuff today or ain't I? You do and sometimes you don't, but there weren't never a time when I cared about doing anything else."

How, then, I asked, did he come to sell out the game he loved?

Well, there it was, out in the open. It just popped out of me. He winced as though I'd dared to slap his face, and he tried to conceal his uneasiness by bringing the Scotch to his lips. For a moment, I was afraid I had blown it all, that he would finish his drink and ask me to leave. I sat there waiting, nervously sipping mine, wanting to pull my words back, to wipe them out of the air the way one might erase a dirty word on a blackboard.

"It was a crazy time," he said. "I don't know how it happened, but it did, all right. I've thought about it plenty over the years and I don't know. Maybe it was one of those God-awful things that just happen to you. You don't know what you're doing, then one day you wake up and it's there, real as life. I guess that comes from being dumb. God damn, I was dumb, all right. Old Gandil was smart and the rest of us was dumb. We started out gabbing about all the big money we would take, like a bunch of kids pretending to be big shots, you know? It just seemed like a bunch of talk. I never really believed it would happen. I don't think any of us even wanted it to happen, 'cept Gandil. But it happened, all right. Gandil gave Cicotte ten grand the night before the opener, and the next thing we knew, we were all tied up in it."

He described the sinister background of the fix, how "there was so much crookedness around, you sort of fell into it," laughing at a sudden memory. "Once, when I was playing factory ball, some guy calls to me in the outfield—they stood around the fence out there, you know. He shows me this gun he's packing and he said, 'Oscar, I want you to drop the next fly ball comes your way!' I couldn't believe it, but the next inning, some guy hits a long one to center and I got to thinking, That crazy coot is gonna shoot me!"

"Did you make the catch?" I asked.

"Are you kidding? The thing stopped rolling halfway to the fence, and I kicked it the rest of the way."

He talked a lot about Comiskey, what a penny pincher he was. "He gave us three dollars a day meal money on the road. Jesus, even the A's in last place got four dollars. It wasn't just the low salaries." In mid-July, they had gotten together and asked for a bonus in response to their greatness as a team, plus the record attendance figures—then, failing that, they had threatened to strike. But Comiskey had remained defiant, contemptuous, even. "You couldn't get with a man like that."

He poured it all out, reliving his anger like one who had kept it bottled up for too long. There was something pathetic about the way he kept shaking his head, apologizing for what they had done. Yet it seemed to me that all those reasons for the fix, however valid, were not *his* reasons, that he had absorbed the thinking of others and had made it his own. He had simply gone along with Gandil and the others, I suspected, selling away his career for the $5,000 he received without really wanting to be involved.

Nonetheless, he *had* played to lose, at least in some of the games. He took me through the entire Series, play by play, explaining what he had done in this game or that, or what he knew he had failed to do. He barely mentioned the other seven, not wanting to talk about them, and I did not pursue it. "Playing rotten, it ain't that hard to do when you get the hang of it. It ain't that hard to hit a pop-up while you take what looks like a good cut at the ball." Then he added, "It ain't that much fun, neither." He confessed he had helped to throw games during the 1920 season as well, just as Red Faber had said. And when I asked him why, he couldn't answer. He just swallowed thickly, looking terribly helpless.

"The way I heard it, you were afraid of the gamblers," I said. "Was that true?"

He wouldn't answer that, either. I got the feeling he was all talked out, and, finally, I prepared to leave.

"You know the biggest regret?" His smile reflected a more joyous conclusion to the day. "I got kicked out of baseball the year they souped up the ball. Why, I could've hit forty homers with that lively ball! Like Ruth!"

A week later, I called to find out how he was feeling. He was sleeping, and Mrs. Felsch told me he was about the same. She also told me that it was true about the gamblers, they *had* frightened him. They had threatened to hurt the children. They had six children. It was something he never spoke of, she said.

In many ways his story was typical. He had given the core of his life away in a feeble, senseless gesture, then was intimidated into a pathetic silence until I reached him a few years before he died. For forty years, he had lived in shame, not because others abused him, but because he had been a fool, they had all been fools, suckered into an idiotic deal they did not even want. He never saw his compatriots after their eventual retirement, nor did any of them care to contact him. It was as though they had all tainted each other and preferred to live apart from the entire experience.

Only Felsch had talked, or so it turned out.

Seven years later, in May 1969, I received a call from Lee Allen, official historian of baseball's Hall of Fame in Cooperstown, New York, informing me that Ed Cicotte was dying and the word was out that he wanted to talk.

I went to Detroit the following day, but the old pitcher was in a coma, and a day later, he died.

Mrs. Cicotte was kind enough to tell me that her husband had read *Eight Men Out* (I'd sent him a copy) and thought it was "a very fine book."

The trip, then, was not a total waste.

19.

What is a book, anyway?

The word itself has achieved a variety of meanings and usages. "She's tops in my book" . . . "This is one for the books" . . . "I'd make book on that" . . . "They'll throw the book at you" . . . "He was brought to book" . . . "They booked a room at a hotel" . . . "I've got to call my bookie".

It would seem that the answer depends on who is being asked. I once heard a publisher liken a book to horse manure. To its creator, the horse, it is obviously something far different than to a stableboy, its recipient. And to a farmer in need of fertilizer, it is something else again.

As for a book, a reader might think of it as an entertainment or a source of knowledge or a stimulant to his imagination. To a publisher—whatever else he might say of it—it is primarily a piece of merchandise.

To a writer, however, the answer is far more personal and

infinitely more involved. For me, with the Black Sox Scandal, my book was an adventure in itself, the consummation of many months' work demanding more concentrated man-hours than any factory hand amassed even in wartime. More significantly, it had become an important part of my education, for I had come to understand a complex set of forces that represented a continuing theme in American history. I had set it down like one transferred in time, as if I'd actually been there in 1919, living among them, listening to them talk, feeling their frustrations, absorbing their rage, sharing their venality. All this was not a contrivance; it was the way I actually came to know it.

To determine the next phase were the editors, in this case, Howard Cady's replacement at Putnam's: Peter Israel, editor in chief, and Harvey Ginsberg, senior editor.

A week or so after my submission, they saw fit to reject it. No requests for rewrite, not even an editorial comment. Harvey said simply, politely: "Sorry, I'm afraid it isn't what we expected."

I took the manuscript over to Howard Cady at Holt, Rinehart and Winston, struggling to contain any lack of confidence.

Three or four days later, Howard called me from Washington, D.C.

"It's just fine!" he said with quiet enthusiasm. He would see to it that my Putnam's contract would be bought by Holt. He was absolutely delighted about the prospects.

Well, all right, I thought. Jesus Christ, yes. Wow! I mean, I confess that I'd really begun to sweat.

The new contract arrived for my signature, then the check for $1,250, the second half of my advance. Acceptance was cause for rejoicing. (I took the rest of the day off.) When I bothered to figure out my finances on this project, however, I realized it had cost me over $4,000 in travel expenses alone—to say nothing of living expenses for the eighteen months since I began. To put it conservatively, the book had cost me around $12,000.

Still, one had to figure that the rewards were yet to come.

"There'll be some editing on your book, Eliot," Howard said. "I'll get back to you in a week or so."

"Fine," I replied, then added a note that I had not yet selected a satisfactory title. *The Black Sox Scandal*, perhaps. Or, more simply, *The Black Sox?*

"There's time enough for that," Howard assured me.

A week went by, then another, then still another, but he did not call. And when he did, it was to report that "There are problems, Eliot," his quiet, friendly manner somewhat more subdued than usual. "The legal department feels the book might be litigious."

"What seems to be the trouble?" I asked. "I mean, which parts bothered them?"

The silence that followed was devastating. The word that broke the silence was even more so.

"Everything," was all he said.

I was to bring in all my sources, the entire compilation of published material I'd used, the thousands of pages of notes, tape recordings—everything, in fact. I spent a day and a half sorting it all, packing it into a large corrugated box, then delivered it to Howard.

Once again, I would have to wait.

It was a highly unenviable position. To have one's fate in the hands of unseen lawyers, whose responsibility to the corporation is most readily demonstrated by saying no (and taking a long time about it, if only to indicate the thoroughness of their preparation), is to learn how to suffer. Almost a month went by before Howard called me again.

Could I come to lunch on the following Monday? It seemed that Al Edwards, president of Holt, Rinehart and Winston, wanted to meet me. Howard tried to explain: "I'm sorry, but I think it's because he wants to apologize."

Meaning, to reject the book.

It is at such moments that the psyche is so severely wrenched, the body goes out of control. I broke into a sweat, beads of it erupting all over me, and I could feel every one of them, evil little bugs crawling down my face, under my shirt, into my socks. Then, too, my stomach began to churn, the ultimate barometer of my anguish, and I bet

$100 to a dime I'd be spending the night nursing an extended bout of diarrhea.

The name of the game was fear.

They were flushing away my book, and there wasn't a bloody thing I could do about it.

Only once before in my life had I felt anything so terrifying. Ten years before, in 1952, I was just beginning to make good as a writer, a husband, a father, even. I was gaining a foothold in television as a promising young writing talent in those oncoming, so-called Golden Years, when suddenly I was told the bad news:

Blacklisted.

The one-word wipeout.

It was the time of that snarling tarantula named Senator Joseph McCarthy and his red-baiting crusade against the alleged omnipresence of Communists in all walks of American life. It was the time when television networks and sponsors and ad agencies crumbled before the arbitrary threats of a solitary grocer in Syracuse, New York, named Lawrence Johnson, lest he remove their toothpaste or laundry soap or canned soups from his shelves. It was a time when actors, writers, directors saw their entire careers become nothing.

If one was named as a "subversive," that was the end. It didn't matter what the justifications—or the lack of them—or who said what to whom. Besides, there was no way to find out.

It wasn't until years later that I came to know a government agent who pulled out my FBI file for a look-see. I was staggered to learn that the sole reference to my subversiveness was a petition I had signed in 1951, outside Yankee Stadium, urging the New York Yankees to hire a Negro ballplayer.

Again, baseball.

Now, in 1962, I told Howard Cady that I didn't care to meet Mr. Edwards. The head of Holt, Rinehart and Winston was, I had heard, a banker, not an editor. What was the point of such a meeting? Howard replied that it could very well be important since Mr. Edwards requested it.

"To kiss me off, that's why!" I said.

"Maybe," Howard replied. "But I just don't see how we can afford to miss hearing him out."

Al Edwards was an extremely likable gentleman. As we sat sipping Bloody Marys in the spacious Grill of the Hotel Roosevelt, he spoke with great pride of having published Robert Frost's poetry in many editions, as well as several books about Frost's life and work. As a result, Holt had practically cornered the market of Frostiana. I commented on my own affection for the great New England poet. I had spent some time in New England, not only as a boy at summer camp, a year at semipro baseball, but also my freshman year at Williams College in Massachusetts. I even told Mr. Edwards that I had met Mr. Frost there.

He perked up at that, sensing a piece of conversation that would forestall the inevitable moment of truth.

"You met him? Tell me about it," he said.

"Well, he came to Williams to read his poetry, and naturally, I went to hear him. When he finished, he invited us to leave our own poems with the dean; he said he'd be happy to read them—and comment. I had written a few, so I dared."

Mr. Edwards kept nodding, urging me on. "Yes . . . ? You gave him your poems . . . Yes?" as though I were telling a story of enormous suspense.

"Well, the next morning, I was summoned to the dean's office, and sure enough, there was Frost. There were six or seven of us fledgling poets."

"Did he read your poems?"

"One of them. He read it aloud. Right there."

"Oh, my. Your poem! He read your poem! Do you still happen to have it somewhere? That poem?"

"Mr. Edwards, I could not possibly forget it. Ever."

I proceeded to recite it, staring into my drink to avoid my embarrassment.

> *Winter has no rhythm, friend,*
> *No lilting forms, no supple ways;*

Besieged, we let its curse offend
And dissipate a hundred days.

Songs of cryo joys, they'll sing,
Of heaven on a frosty glaze,
But don't believe the lies they bring,
Their heaven's where the devil plays.

It's sun, I crave, and springy sod
To run on spikes, to hit and throw,
It's baseball, friend, that shows me God,
I'd opt for hell to make it so.

Mr. Edwards could hardly contain his smile. "That's absolutely fascinating," he said. "Did he like it?"

"I was afraid you'd ask me that," I replied.

"What did he say?"

"Well, he sized me up for a few seconds, then he shook his head. 'It's a pop fly, son,' he said."

Mr. Edwards laughed. "He said that? 'It's a pop fly'?"

I nodded, and we all laughed together.

Mr. Edwards wanted to know more about me. I told him that the poem had been significant, how baseball had been an extremely meaningful part of my life. He seemed extremely sensitive to the thrust of this, probing into my background like one who found all this extraordinary. And when we were sipping coffee at its end, he suddenly let out a bombshell.

"Howard," he said, finally turning his attention to the editor in chief, "I believe we ought to publish this young man's book."

20.

It was beautiful to be a winner, but I had lingering doubts about its validity, for I simply could not trust a victory brought on by a pop-fly poem. It seemed too capricious, a victory without substance that would doubtlessly sag like a sand castle at the first slap of a wave.

I'd once heard a story about an aging French folk singer working in a smoky Left Bank bistro. It was an especially bad night for him: he had no energy, his throat was sore, his fingers were clumsy on the guitar. At the end of his set, however, the crowd of kids applauded vociferously, stamping and cheering with genuine appreciation. The singer turned to his bass player in rueful comment: "Huh," he sighed, "another shitty victory."

I had just won one, hadn't I.

There was, however, no need for me to be rueful about it. I had a right to a few lucky breaks. Sometimes, line drives get caught and handle hits drop in. As ballplayers like to say of the latter: "They look just like line drives in the box scores."

So much of life was like that, it was bewildering.

A matter of how the cookie crumbles.

Indeed, it was all tied up in the question Al Edwards had asked me: "Eliot, how did you ever get to be a writer?"

I had ducked the answer; it was simply too involved. The truth was, it came about by a series of defeats and flukes and crazy bounces.

To explain the genesis of most writers is like paddling a canoe upstream with a tennis racket. In my case, there was precious little to have forecast it. I had never nursed any youthful ambitions to be a writer, nor had I any deep affinity for literature. In school, my preference had been for history. Had I taken any psychological tests for aptitude, I might have indicated a leaning toward teaching. As it turned out, I'd moved through young adulthood without any direction, propelled by a bizarre series of accidents in a chain of seemingly unrelated events, one leading to another until, at the age of thirty, I ended up alone with a typewriter.

The first fluke, one might say, happened in the spring of 1943. As a soldier, I had spent fifteen months in the infantry, then washed out of flying-cadet school and ended up in a relatively pleasant job at Maxwell Field, Alabama, as a physical-training instructor. I was living comfortably in a dormitory, the food was far superior to any I'd had elsewhere in the service, weekend passes were freely available. We were coming into baseball season, and I'd been asked to organize a post team, perhaps even to manage it, a prospect that seemed almost as exciting as winning the war. I had found a home, as they said in those days, and fantasized about sitting out the duration in highly agreeable indolence.

Then came Hank Greenberg.

The great Detroit Tiger slugger had dropped out of baseball in the spring of 1941, volunteering for duty six months before Pearl Harbor was hit. As a major attached to the Fourth Technical Training Command operating out of Texas, he toured the area on periodic inspections for the purpose of improving training programs.

He was the only major-league baseball player I knew, the connection being a onetime pinochle game between his father and my uncle. Years before, we had met a few times, the young aspiring fan and the great star. At the time, I think he appreciated me mostly for not bothering him for autographs.

When he approached me I was conducting calisthenics on the raised platform barking out commands with resounding crispness to a squadron spread out in front of me. When I finished the session, he came over to greet me.

"You're in fine voice, Eliot," he kidded me.

"I was always a pretty good bench jockey," I noted.

"Shower up and meet me in the officers' club," he said.

"I can't go there, Hank," I replied. "I'm not an officer."

He was stunned. With mounting disapproval he looked at me for what seemed like a long time. Then he threw at me what I would later learn to call "The Jesus Speech."

"We're in a war, Eliot. I don't need to tell you how serious that is . . ."

"I'm doing my job," I said.

"A man with your background and education . . . the army needs good officers. You're a waste doing this . . ."

I said nothing, tasting the guilt rising in my throat. There was no room for rebuttal here.

"You'll go on the next OSC list." He offered his hand, I shook it, and we parted.

Three weeks later, I was shipped to the air force officer candidate school in Miami Beach, and after ninety days of unmitigated chickenshit, I was commissioned as a second lieutenant.

That was August 1943. By Christmas, I was sitting on what had to be rated as one of the worst tours of duty in air force history: the Aleutian Islands.

On Adak, the first desolate rock to become my home for the following two years, I wrote Major Henry Greenberg a brief, sardonic note to thank him for this phase of his contribution to the war effort.

Needless to say, he did not bother to acknowledge it.

What seems so incredible now, however, was the way those next twenty-eight months managed to change my life.

James Jones, the war hater/lover novelist, dedicated *The Thin Red Line* "To those greatest and most heroic of all human endeavors, War and Warfare, may they never cease to give us the pleasure, excitement, and adrenal stimulation we need. . . ."

In the Aleutians, war was sheer boredom. By the time I'd arrived, the Japanese had been wiped off the Aleutian chain, and the only enemy left was ourselves. Baseball seemed too distant to contemplate. Whatever ball fans there were seemed determined to avoid mention of it lest it somehow sully the purity of their memories. (A religious man is not apt to discuss God in a bordello.) For the first extended time in my life, I forgot about the game.

The war, or at least this sordid fringe of it, became the core of my concern. I was not going to be one who lived in memories. I would burn all those bridges. And while I had no vision of the future to replace it, I became deeply involved in what was going on around me—and that was my salvation.

I took over as a special service officer, initiating an extensive information and education program. As a result of this, I began to read seriously. And so it was that I met Dashiell Hammett, a fifty-five-year-old corporal who, far more than I, knew how to plunge into the present. Hammett had joined up to get into the fight, even if it meant living on this desolate island. (Had the War Department sent him to this American Siberia out of fear of what they considered to be his radical impact?) He became editor and mentor of the *Adakian,* the post newspaper, an appealing four-page multigraphed daily that everybody read and most everybody loved. He worked hard, brilliantly, in fact, an inspiration to many fledgling journalists who worked with him.

I was twenty-four years old, and I sat at his feet. In the process, I was thrown together with others who were infinitely better informed than I. For the first time in my life I began to think seriously about something other than myself.

On Adak, as everywhere, there was plenty to see and much to learn. Men totally without women or purpose (or even whisky) occupied the lonely months initiating flimflams, stealing supplies, gambling, and going mad. A society dedicated to petty rapaciousness wherein the distinction between officers and enlisted men was strictly a matter of style. Inevitably, I would collect the most gruesome victimizations.

For example, the time when the base commander selfishly appropriated the huge hot-water boiler that had been requisitioned to replace the faulty one in the enlisted men's only shower room. A few weeks after, I witnessed the grotesque result: an explosion in the old boiler wherein two showering GIs were blown to bits. As it turned out, the colonel readily covered up a scandal by simply ordering the removal of all traces of the shower room itself before the inspector general arrived on the scene.

Repelled by such venalities, I would occasionally pass them on to Hammett. Sam, as we called him (his full name was Samuel Dashiell Hammett), had experienced worse in his time.

"Everybody knows *what*," he said. "The real question is *why*?"

Nonetheless, he relished my indignation, or so I gauged it, for he would twinkle when I came into the *Adakian* Quonset in those late hours after the paper had been put to bed. "Well, well, who got screwed today?" he would tease me, and I would continue with my litany of horrors.

One night, a small USO troop came to perform at the airbase, its provocative torch singer in a low-cut gown seductively moaning "Embrace me, my sweet embraceable you" to a flustered GI she had plucked from the audience, teasing us all as she gyrated against him on stage, her soft hands stroking his neck, her body rubbing against his. Choked with envy, my throat locked in anguish while others stomped and whistled as the soldier made his move, his hands clutching her bare back then dipping to the curve of her buttocks, and his mouth burrowed into her neck as he locked his body to hers. And when she finished the song, he kissed her with a ferocity that demanded all of her, her terror evident as she struggled for release. I had never seen rape, and certainly not through the pulse of the rapist, but suddenly there it was, as large as life, and I gasped in horror, my hot body shaking uncontrollably, needing his victory more than I'd ever needed my own. It was a moment of such obsession, I did not know myself; there was no link to life but a driving pain in my loins, an incredible roaring in my ears. It ended only when the MPs leaped on stage, brutally aborting the act with flailing sticks as the audience screamed in protest.

An entertainment?

It was a night that ended with one soldier almost killing another after a homosexual attack.

All this I told to Hammett and the others, doubtlessly wallowing in an emotion I knew I would never forget. Hammett sat hidden behind the smoke from his cigarette and said nothing. It was not until several days later that I heard his reaction from someone else.

"Yeah, he said it was too damn bad you weren't a writer."

Such a line is nothing more than a throwaway, but it lingered in memory to be used when I needed it. When the war ended, I began to nurse fantasies about setting it all down. I might even have tried if it weren't for Norman Mailer's *The Naked and the Dead*, a book so overwhelming, I could not bear to face my own amateurishness.

But what to do with my life? It was a measure of my postwar confusion that the capricious chain of events that led to the typewriter should now reverse directions—or, at least, appear to.

It was spring 1946, and, totally without portfolio, I found myself drifting back into baseball. I returned to the New England league where I had played so promisingly when in college, immediately finding acceptance with the Montpelier (Vermont) Club, managed by an ex–Big League pitcher named Ray Fisher, who, I would later realize, had actually pitched against the 1919 Chicago White Sox in that fateful World Series. (Also on this team was a nineteen-year-old college hopeful named Robin Roberts.) I had no prospect of making a comeback, but merely sought the pleasure of one more season on spikes. An old-timer at the age of twenty-six who had not played ball for five years, I failed to get in shape quickly enough, pulling a groin muscle running out an infield hit my very first time at bat. I knew I was through.

Back in New York, I hit on another idea: I would own my own semipro team in New York's Metropolitan Baseball Association. If I could no longer play, I would promote. I settled in Yonkers, then went after the best ballplayers I could find—including Mickey Rutner, offering him more money than he could make in the AAA Texas League, but it was not in him to abandon his dream of making the majors. I even pursued Max Lanier, the great left-handed pitcher from the St. Louis Cardinals who had defected to the Mexican League and was barred from professional baseball as a result. We came to terms, all right, only to discover the awesome power of the major-league-baseball establishment, who saw to it that any association with Lanier would lead to total ostracism, even among semiprofessional clubs.

Nonetheless, I put together a strong team that included one ex-major leaguer, Nick Tremark, of the 1938 Dodgers. I was back on spikes, though primarily as a manager, loving every minute of it. For a season, it was marvelous fun if unprofitable business. We were strong enough to compete against the best black teams, at a time when Jackie Robinson was the only black in the majors. We would figure out how to pitch to such sluggers as Luke Easter (slow stuff) and defend against Orestes Minoso (pray). We'd try delayed steals and double squeeze plays. I had my club playing the kind of baseball I grew up on. As a result, winning far more one-run games than losing.

It was also the year that Mickey Rutner finally made it to the majors, if only for a cup of coffee, as they say: a dozen games with Connie Mack's A's at the end of the 1947 season. I went to Yankee Stadium to see him pump two sharp hits off the great Joe Page, drive in the winning run, then start a crisp double play that saved the win in the bottom of the ninth.

We had a beer together in a nearby pub, and Mickey was glowing with the triumphant sense of the day, the fabulous demonstration of his skills, Yankee Stadium itself—it was all of a piece. He had come a long way through years of frustration in the minors, and now it seemed as though it had all been worth the struggle.

"You looked like an old pro," I said.

"I felt good, all right."

"I watched you work at the plate. You knew you were going to hit him, didn't you."

"I was tight at first. But it's wonderful the way you can rely on what you know. I told myself that there never was a pitcher I couldn't hit. I don't care what they throw at me, I can always get a piece of the ball. I just wasn't going to let him throw it by me . . ."

"You hit him like you owned him, Mick . . ."

We drank beer in silence for a moment. I could see how happy he was.

"I can play in the majors, El."

"I always thought that."

"I know I can."

As it turned out, the A's had no room for him, and Mickey was worth more to them in the Texas League than bait for trading. He was good, but at twenty-eight they didn't think he was good enough.

Both Rutner and I (and, coincidentally, Hank Greenberg) finally hung up our spikes that year. My own club folded along with the entire Metropolitan Baseball Association (and most of the minor leagues) under the impact of television: who, in their right mind, would pay a dollar or more to watch Asinof et al., when they could see DiMaggio, Robinson, Mize, et al. for free?

Another crumbling of the cookie.

I was twenty-eight years old; after three years in baseball and almost five more in the army, what was I worth to any potential employer? When I found work, it was as a salesman, first in advertising, then finally in my family's clothing business. Dutifully, I went on the road to sell, putting in several hundred miles a day, spurred by the rewards of making money, by the idea that my acceptance of such an orientation was a sign of maturity, that happiness would be a house in Mamaronek.

It was a delusion. I gravitated, not toward Westchester County, but toward the Broadway theater. I spent my money on Tennessee Williams, Arthur Miller, Elmer Rice, Maxwell Anderson, and dozens of plays with serious provocative themes. I saw them all, then read them and hung out with people who talked about them, for they were far more stimulating than the sharkskin worsteds in the fall line.

Then, too, it was a time of political turmoil: Winston Churchill's "Iron Curtain" speech at Fulton, Missouri, and the onset of the cold war, Henry Wallace and the Progressive party, Harry Truman and the Korean War; and I found myself drawn into the vortex of political protest. In this setting, at a fund-raising party for Henry Wallace's bid for the presidency, I met Jocelyn Brando, an actress who, at the time, had the only female part in *Mister Roberts*. Having grown up dating wealthy Jewish girls whose lives were devoted to finding wealthy Jewish husbands (the sort of prospective wife I'd long since learned to run away from), I found Jocelyn like a woman from another continent. She was, of course, exactly what I needed— while she, surfeited with the madness of theater people, wanted the stability represented by a businessman.

Meanwhile, like that dying salesman Willie Loman, I found myself driving dangerously onto road shoulders. And one night, in Butler, Pennsylvania, I woke up in a hotel room without the vaguest notion of where I was or what I was doing. Frightened, I drove home and quit.

It was definitely a time of crisis.

What was I going to do?

I was thirty years old with a history of failures and totally without portfolio. I had no known workable talents or skills. My head was loaded with an endless list of careers and professions and jobs I summarily rejected. My decision, then, erupted from my fantasies. When I spoke it aloud to Jocelyn, it was as if to convince myself of its efficacy. And even as I did, I sensed I had no right to take on such a challenge. Indeed, I half expected her to laugh, or at least be shocked.

"I'm going to write . . ." I said.

"Yes, you should . . ." she said, leaving myself as the shocked one.

I had written a story once, an assignment during my freshman year at Williams College. A week later, the instructor announced he was selecting two stories from the group, one an example of excellence, and the other, as he put it, "an abomination." He then proceeded to read the latter first: mine, as it turned out. And though he graciously omitted the author's name, my humiliation left me choking.

For openers, then, it was hardly an inspiring memory on which to launch a career. But this was a dozen years later, I told myself, and even the great Willie Mays didn't get a base hit for the first fourteen times he went to bat with the New York Giants.

Resolutely, I sat at the typewriter and wrote a short story. Inevitably, it was about the only thing I really knew: baseball. It dealt with the emotions of a ballplayer like my friend Mickey Rutner, finally coming up for a chance at the Big Leagues after being kicked around the minors for a dozen years.

Jocelyn was marvelously supportive. She'd hear me pecking away and remark how pleasing the sound of it was. I'd hear her tell friends that I was a writer—and I'd love the sound of that. To be a writer—it was something to be in awe of. I pipe-dreamed making a living as one. Meanwhile, friends looked glumly at me and felt sorry for Jocelyn. ("He can always go back into the clothing business," they assured her.) Nor did it make matters any simpler that her younger brother, an actor named Marlon, was rapidly becoming an incredible success. I could even sense his embarrassment to see his sister saddled with a thirty-year-old amateur for a husband. He saw the complexity of my marriage, how dramatically its balance had shifted as a result of this folly of mine, how it must have shaken her.

"It's like ordering a chicken-salad sandwich and getting a BLT," Marlon said to me.

"Well, she likes BLT," I offered.

"Not without bacon," he countered.

Which, of course, was what a husband was supposed to bring home, and I no longer was.

He had a gift for the metaphor, frequently getting at the essence of a person by describing the weather or a necktie or a piece of music. Years later, he would describe me as "a maroon-and-gray Mercury three-door sedan with seventy-five thousand miles on it, slow to start in cold weather, but it gets you there, though one of the tires has a slow leak (it needs to be pumped up frequently), one of the directional signals doesn't work, and the horn blows 'ha ha.' "

He could also challenge you while belittling himself.

"How many fingers do you type with?" he asked me.

"Two," I said, raising my index fingers.

He looked skeptical. "Is that enough?"

"Well, it's just a short story," I quipped.

"But you have to clip those two nails?"

"Yeah, I guess."

He was enormously sympathetic at that. "I could never

be a writer," he said. "Those are my nose-picking fingers."

For three weeks, then, I didn't pick my nose—and finished what I felt to be a worthwhile effort. It was called "The Rookie." I sent it to Vance Bourjaily, distinguished novelist and playwright, then assembling material for *Discovery*, an anthology of new writing. Since he was a friend, I knew I would get a fair and prompt reading.

Indeed, a few days later he called.

"Let's talk about this," he said, and invited me to his apartment doubling as an office.

Vance was friendly, totally honest, extremely bright. His first words out of the box were memorable: "Your story is terrible. It's terrible for the worst possible reason: you simply don't know how to write." Then he spelled it out, paragraph by paragraph, explaining how I failed to construct properly, used words poorly, muddled my ideas with foolish phrases and false images. He worked me over for almost an hour, referring to the extensive notes he had made in the margins as well as innumerable red-lined words.

His summation was sympathetic but devastating.

"Really, El . . . I seriously suggest you go back to the clothing business."

Through it all, I kept a brave face out of fear that he'd lie to me, for the last thing I wanted was to be stroked. When we finished, I thanked him with the profuseness of one whose life had just been spared. My stomach was gurgling audibly, that old sign of unmanageable crisis. I hurried out of his apartment as if a bomb were about to detonate.

If I were a drinking man, I would have rushed to the nearest bar. I ended up in Central Park—across from an active ball field, no less— on a bench I shall always remember. I reread the story, reliving the impact of every comment Vance had made. Then I reread it again, slowly savoring his notes, and I began to see what he meant. I sat there for another hour, then started to find new words, new images to set the stage. "The Rookie walked into the batter's circle listening to the clamor of the largest crowd he'd ever seen. He was unable to resist looking up at the towering stadium that enveloped him . . ."

It sounded so right, I stopped, needing this small salve to my shattered ego. I tucked the story in my pocket and started the long walk home, swearing that I would not go back to the clothing business. I was going to sell "The Rookie" if I had to rewrite it a dozen more times.

Three weeks later, I sent it back to Vance without comment. He called a day later, sounding confused but playful.

"All right, El, who wrote it?"

No accusation of deviousness intended: it was merely his way of passing on the good news. We met again for another round of editing, but this time it was sheer pleasure.

Discovery bought my story for $125.

A beginning. Not lucrative, but auspicious. No longer a pop-fly poet, I could swing away with a little confidence.

To make a living, however, was a whole other ball game, and logically enough, I gravitated to where the money was: television.

To get assignments in television, one needs a credit. To get a credit, one needs a sale. To get a sale, one needs the right idea for the right show and the right moment. I wrote dozens of shows on speculation; several were near misses, but none were takers.

Then came the fluke that turned the tide.

The result of a poker game, no less. Between hands, a friend remarked that NBC had recently decided to convert that eerie radio show "Lights Out" into a televison series, and that Larry Schwab, producer-director, was desperately looking for scripts. Did I write stuff about supernatural horrors?

"Certainly," I lied.

I was to join him and Schwab for lunch the very next day—with an outline.

It was Jocelyn's idea, fittingly conceived that night in the dreary hours before dawn: a house in Salem, Massachusetts, was possessed by a vampire witch, a house that drank the blood of its tenants (a vacationing young artistic couple from Greenwich Village) and actually bled when its walls were punctured. Would the couple discover this before the house did them in?

They bought it. Four hundred dollars for a half-hour show to be written for live performance barely three weeks later.

The script was properly ghoulish enough, but what appeared on screen transcended all horror. The dramatic crisis of the last act was, of course, the hero's discovery of the house's bloody secret; this to be revealed as he drives a nail into the wall to hang his wife's new painting, and faces the grotesque sight of blood oozing from the puncture.

To effect this startling image, I'd suggested that a syringe filled with dark liquid be mounted behind the wall, whereupon the driven nail would release the flow. A tight camera shot, first on the "bleeding" wall and then on the actor's face, would tell it all. At dress rehearsal, I saw that three stagehands had set up a huge pumping contraption from which a long tube was joined to the wall, but it could not be tested for fear of soiling the set before air time. I questioned the effectiveness of this unecessarily complicated device, but was assured it would do the job.

An hour or so later, at home, we watched the show build to this crucial climactic moment. When the actor pounded the nail, however, the blood did not ooze, it squirted with startling power, spraying him like a fire hose, all but knocking him off his feet! The whole show, of course, went with it.

"Welcome to the wonderful world of television," said a friend.

It was horrible. We laughed, but everything was pain. I cringed at this first public sight of my name and brooded for days. I even wrote my first piece of doggerel since college:

> *A man's ambition must be mighty lean*
> *To seek his name on the video screen.*

Months later, I chanced to meet the unfortunate actor on a bus, and since he did not recognize me, it seemed like a fertile moment for a summing up.

"Say, didn't I see you on a weird TV show?" I asked.

He scowled, then uncorked the sordid details.

"Yeah, and I'm suing NBC over it."

"How come?" I asked.

"That goo they sprayed on me ruined a good suit and gave me a skin infection that kept me from working for over a month!"

Commiserating, I asked how a thing like that could have happened.

"It was the pump they had behind the wall. A stagehand told me they wanted to use a simple syringe that would drip the blood, but the writer insisted on the pump."

What followed over the years was not much better, though I began to make a decent living. Television was moving into the Golden Years and the prospects seemed highly encouraging. I was even learning to type with four fingers.

Then, suddenly, jarringly, almost without warning, I was blacklisted. A television producer at CBS simply told me that he could no longer hire me.

Within a month, Jocelyn was told exactly the same thing.

You can knock a writer out of television, but you cannot still his typewriter. However, to bar an actress from the largest part of her audience is to leave her dangling in limbo. Jocelyn, like many others, was jerked off balance. The satisfactions of her career were tenuous enough—like treading water in a turbulent sea—but the blacklist pinned her arms to her sides. If there were still theatrical jobs to be won, working television actresses would inevitably get them. The system tends not to award its victims.

I raged at this inequity. Like Marlon, she was represented by MCA, the largest entertainment-business agency in the world, but she found no work. Since MCA controlled several TV shows, I even began to suspect that they were deliberately keeping her off the screen to avoid drawing any attention to Marlon's golden name, for he, too, was in jeopardy. Indeed, to clear him for the MGM production of *Julius Caesar*, I would subsequently hear of million-dollar payoffs to blacklisting power groups.

As for me, it could be said that the blacklist turned into a blessing. No more bleeding walls or other insults, I went to work on a novel. Again, it was Vance Bourjaily who opened that door.

"This character you wrote about in 'The Rookie,'" he began. "There's a novel there someplace, a serious novel about what it's really like to be a ballplayer, not the usual romantic nonsense."

My head went high with the thought of it. To write a novel would be like trying to climb Mr. Everest.

"Just consider what's actually been written about baseball," he went on. "It's all a lot of froth from the outsider's point of view. Starting with Lardner, for example, and all those who emulated his style. Mark Harris's *The Southpaw*. Or even Bernie Malamud's *The Natural*, a skillful collage of baseball myths. He doesn't get at the game itself. How could he? He doesn't know baseball. Melville could never have written *Moby Dick* if he hadn't actually lived as a whaler. I doubt if Malamud ever wore spikes. But you have, El. And it obviously meant a lot to you. Why don't you try it?"

Yes, why didn't I?

I was thoroughly intimidated, that was why.

Then I reread *The Natural, The Southpaw, The Year the Yankees Lost the Pennant,* and I saw what Bourjaily meant. They were fables about baseball, not baseball at all. They were using baseball to tell stories. As I saw it, the need was for a book that dealt realistically with the oppressive system under which ballplayers had to play. No one had ever written a novel about life in the minor leagues, about how a marginal ballplayer (like Mickey Rutner) had to play at a salary dictated by his club owner or not play at all—indeed, where the player was owned outright and in perpetuity.

I discussed all this with Mickey and began to see the potential. After telling me his experience, he steered me to others, and from there I went to the *Congressional Record*, eventually to the unsuccessful court cases that challenged organized baseball's inviolate status as a sport not a business.

"Too bad he's not a writer," Hammett had said.

By God, I would write not only *Moby Dick* but Upton Sinclair's *The Jungle!*

But again, I also had to make a living, in this instance, through the good auspices of a motion-picture-and-television fan magazine that paid me $250 per monthly article to profile such diverse luminaries as Julius La Rosa, Wally Cox, Marilyn Monroe, Larry Storch, Grace Kelly. It was not always easy. Marilyn Monroe, for example, was not feeling well at the time but advised me to write the piece anyway. "Make it up," she said. And so I did. Another time, I met Grace Kelly as she was sitting for the portrait photographer Peter Basch, but she refused to talk to me. Since this was an assignment she'd agreed to, I persisted, even following her into a cab (to the MCA offices, as it turned out).

"Would you please tell Jay Kantor that I'm here," she told the receptionist.

Jay, I knew, was also Marlon's agent, so I left the same message. A moment later, he came rushing out, not to welcome Grace but, to our mutual amazement, to greet me—possibly because Marlon's three-year contract was about to run out. In fact, after bidding her to wait, he drew me into his office, where, among other small talk, I told him of the troubles Miss K. was giving me. Jay immediately called her in to reproach her, bidding her to go downstairs with me to the Hotel Madison cocktail lounge, on MCA's account, and tell me everything I cared to know.

She did, charmingly. We even held hands for a while.

Writing the novel was something else again. It took me a year of grueling work to complete six chapters (126 pages), which I sent to Vance with terribly mixed feelings. I was tired, frightened, and more confused than I was prepared to admit. To give the manuscript to a stern critic like Vance had to be a suicidal act. He would tell me how bad I suspected it was, and this time I doubted if I had the capacity to cope. I'd even had a friendly lunch with my uncle who ran the family clothing business, a sort of last-ditch precaution.

Then, a few days later, in the middle of the night, the phone rang. It was Vance, too excited to be concerned with the lateness of the hour.

"I just finished. I can't tell you how good it is. You really caught the feel of it, El. The baseball stuff is excellent!"

He went on like that for a few minutes more. I was too staggered—and elated—to reply. We agreed to meet, and I stumbled back to bed, my head spinning with dreams of glory.

After another year, and a lot of assistance, my manuscript was accepted at McGraw-Hill, then published in the spring of 1955. And, by God, there were critics who wrote some marvelously satisfying words, like John Lardner: ". . . an eloquent, moving account." And James T. Farrell: ". . . [The author] conveys a genuine love for the game." And John Hutchens: "This is the way it must be down there (in the minors) . . ." It was the sort of stuff that could send a man soaring. But the words I appreciated most came from Mickey Rutner: "Wow, El, it's a damned good book!"

From Greenberg to Hammett to Bourjaily. Through flukes and failures and fortuity, I had become a writer. But the sine qua non had been baseball.

Indeed, the gods would smile upon me that season. After three years on the television blacklist, I even managed to become employable again, the result of a chance meeting at a party. The producer of a Sunday morning religious show on CBS ("Look up and Live") was in desperate trouble putting together an interview with the great jazz musician Lionel Hampton, who had just returned from a visit to the Holy Land. Could I handle this for him immediately? When I explained that I certainly could try but that I was blacklisted, he replied that the sponsoring organization, the National Council of Churches of Christ, did not respect such injustices, that they would go to bat for me at CBS, that I should do the job regardless of credits.

And so it happened. Early on a Sunday morning, a few days later, my name reappeared on the video screen.

Two months later, a pure and respectable citizen again, I went to Hollywood on a deal to write the screenplay for my book *Man on Spikes*.

It was the stuff of dreams. From a frigid New York winter to sunny palm-lined boulevards. My psyche tingled with glamorous prospects. In 1955, Hollywood was still making over three hundred pictures a year. A writer's paradise—if you wanted money, a mansion with a swimming pool, a Jaguar to tool around in. I didn't meet any who didn't. Writers would tease each other with the fantasy that we were using the fruits of screenwriting to buy time for our more serious work. The joke had it that we really intended to take the money and run back to our novels and plays, only to be repeatedly diverted by some new double-the-previous salary that would keep us hooked, each such gilded advance raising our fabulous standards of living as the years went by, until, Chivas Regal in hand, we languished in absolute luxury with just enough sobriety to utter that preposterously feeble challenge: "Some day I'm going to write a novel exposing this town!"

Not untypically, it turned out that the filming of *Man on Spikes* never happened, and I fluttered from one studio to another. Cop pictures, adventure pictures, war pictures, cowboy pictures. We actually wore the appropriate hat as we worked, as if to lend an air of authenticity to the typing. Even the producers seemed to think well of it—until one maverick was discovered wearing a huge dunce cap.

Still, it was fun. It was no great strain to be a whore when the pay was so good. Working writers are a joy to be with. Give a struggling young talent $1,000 a week and watch what a glorious impact it has on his disposition—no matter what junk he agrees to turn his hand to. I seldom heard anyone talk about content. We were craftsmen in a cream-puff factory. Talented New York playwrights ended up writing adolescent horror films. Serious novelists chased after assignments no more inspiring than "Sergeant Preston of the Yukon." Not surprisingly, I suppose, the language of Hollywood did not even include the word *writing*. A writer would say: "I'm *doing* a 'Gunsmoke,'" or "I'm *doing* a meller at Metro." And, typically, we would expend far more energy in pursuit of the job than "doing" it.

Not without reason, then, they call screenwriters "schmucks with typewriters."

With few exceptions, movies were not works of literary quality but manipulations of adolescent images. The director, the camera-man, the actor were the Main Men. The writer merely laid it out for them. If he was highly paid, it was less for his contribution to the picture than for the abuse that was dumped on him. Studio executives loved to dignify their productions with a big-name writer from the theater or publishing world. It made them feel important. "Give us truth, give us beauty!" they pleaded. But when asked what they thought of the script, they'd reply: "I don't know, my chauffeur hasn't read it yet." Everything was diminished by it. When Clifford

Odets, first of several writers to tackle Thomas Mann's *Joseph and His Brothers,* was asked what he was working on, he replied: "I'm doing one of those pictures where the hero signs his name with a feather."

No matter. Writers in quest of glory would keep flocking to Hollywood, thousands more every year, like mercenary soldiers going to battle in distant deadly wars.

To be sure, I was very small potatoes in that sprawling marketplace. The most consequential reference to my name was that I was the brother-in-law of Marlon Brando, a social and professional reference that drove me up the wall. To my all-too-sensitive ears, the implications were ghastly, as if that were the sum and substance of my talents: a smart operator who had made a good marriage and who, because of it, could write his own ticket in Hollywood. It struck me as incredible, the number of times I'd heard myself referred to in this way, and by important people who should have known better. Whatever tribute that might be to Marlon's extraordinary impact on America, it was demeaning to his kin. No doubt Jocelyn, maintaining her family name, suffered this indignity infinitely more than I, not the least of which was the prospect of being hired for a part *because* of it. In her case, she was an extremely talented actress who had achieved a substantial reputation on Broadway years *before* her brother had arrived. In mine, overhanging many prospective assignments was the producer's illusion that I would, at least, get my finished scenario into Marlon's sympathetic hands. In fact, it was stated to me openly, right from the beginning. Once, it was actually part of a proposed step deal: 1. Outline ($2,000). 2. Treatment ($3,500). 3. Show treatment to Brando ($5,000). Etc.

It became so much a problem, a sympathetic comedy-writer friend once accosted Marlon in Chasen's Restaurant, as though struggling to identify him, then said: "Say, aren't you the brother-in-law of Eliot Asinof?" To compound the problem, Marlon told me that the studio executive with whom he was lunching later referred to me as the best of the young science-fiction writers—referring, of course, to Isaac Asimov, another identity that would plague me for years.

Through all this period, I never so much as discussed a work project with Marlon. I suspected that if I ever came to him with an idea, it would embarrass us both, for he would have suspended judgment out of affection, and done everything possible to help me. Already inundated by an endless stream of offers, not only ideas for films but proposals for glamorous resort hotels, sure-thing oil wells, exotic marriages, he didn't need any offers from me. To keep the air clear between us, I assured him that I never would.

"Just as well," he ribbed me. "I don't see myself making a science-fiction picture . . ."

The Brando problem, however, was endless, trickling down into all areas of my life. As with my son, Martin, for example, a sparkling five-year-old tow-headed kid with a highly endearing precociousness. To some, Martin was known as "Little Marlon." The family resemblance, people would say, was unmistakable, riling me with the notion that my son didn't look like me, he looked like Marlon. (There were even those who thought his name was deliberately chosen to sound as much like his uncle's as possible.) Even my mother would say it: "You know, he looks *just* like him!" in a tone that absolutely creamed over the thought.

The word got around. Once, when I was working at Columbia Pictures, I took Marty to lunch at the old Naples Restaurant on Gower Street, where he went table-hopping to visit writers and actors he knew. Later that afternoon, I got a call from an executive of a high-powered agency whom I knew when he was a low-powered agent—one of those insidious leeches who used to call me trying to reach Marlon.

"Eliot . . . was that 'Little Marlon' I met at lunch today?"

My reaction was a slight but telling uneasiness.

"His name is Martin."

"Marvelous boy!"

"Thanks. He is that."

"About five, is he?"

"Five. That's right."

"Yes, that's what he said."

Beat.

"We're packaging 'Dennis the Menace,' you know. I can tell you, Melvin would be absolutely perfect . . ."

"It's not Melvin," I interrupted.

"What?"

"His name is Martin."

"Right, Martin. Well, I can offer you a grand a week. Thirteen weeks guaranteed. No screen test necessary . . ."

"No," I interrupted again. "Thanks, but the answer is no."

"What!"

"I said, no thanks."

"You ought to talk it over with Joyce, Eliot." He seemed stunned. "You want me to call her?"

"Jocelyn," I corrected him.

"Yes. I mean, I really thought I could talk to you."

"You can," I said. "You *are* talking to me."

"Good. Well, talk it over with her. Give me a call tomorrow."

"I'll tell her, but it won't change anything."

When I got home that evening, I greeted Marty with a special tenderness, like one who'd been away for a long time.

"Hello, Melvin," I said. "They tell me you're five years old."

"Five going on six," he corrected me.

I thought, you know, he really *does* look like Dennis the Menace.

"Who's Melvin?" he asked, looking at me strangely.

"Lassie's brother-in-law," I said, then picked him up to hug him.

For some reason, he laughed.

I didn't call the agent, he called me.

"We'll make it twelve-fifty a week," he said.

I laughed. "Forget it," I said.

Apparently, he couldn't. You could even hear him salivating in those high-powered offices. ("Marvelous kid, I tell you. He even looks like Brando. What a package!") He called back again that afternoon with a different ploy.

"Eliot . . ." he began with a new burst of enthusiasm, "you're making eight hundred a week. Am I right?"

"Right." He was very accurate with numbers, at least.

"Suppose we do a little switch here. You'll get the twelve-fifty, and the kid gets the eight hundred."

This was no small thing, for the raise would establish a whole new salary level for me. It would doubtless even lead to my getting a crack at some decent projects. He knew exactly what he was doing, all right.

"Look," I said, "I talked it over with the kid. He doesn't like Dennis the Menace. He thinks Dennis gives kids a bad name."

Beat.

"I don't believe this," he said. Then, finally: "Okay. Fifteen hundred dollars, that's it."

"Sorry."

I figured I was getting to be a real father, having saved my son's life twice now, the first time two years before when he fell into the hotel swimming pool.

Curiously, this wasn't the end of it. A day or so later, another writer at Columbia dropped in at my office, pipe in hand, ostensibly to chat for a few minutes. At first, there was nothing unique about the visit.

Then: "I heard about your son, El. The Dennis the Menace thing . . ."

"Oh? How?"

He mentioned the agent's name, and I remembered the writer was a client there.

"Yeah," I said. "Pretty crazy, isn't it?"

He puffed thoughtfully on his pipe, then laid his little number on me. "I really don't think it's crazy at all," he began, then went into a long pitch about how child actors weren't any more screwed up than most kids; it depended on the individual, the home, the parents. He even felt it would be good for Marty, make him more responsive to discipline; kids need that these days. "Really, El, you're blowing a big opportunity, not only for the boy but for yourself!"

I thought, if I had a pipe to suck on, I wouldn't have to bite my lip to conceal my disgust. As politely as I could, I asked if the agent had put him up to this talk.

"Well, as a matter of fact, he *did* suggest it . . . But that's certainly not why I'm here, El, you've got to believe *that*, for Chrissakes. Believe me, I *really* think you're making a big mistake."

Sure. The Good Samaritan, Hollywood-style.

I often wondered what the agent was going to do for *him*.

I suppose the story ended fifteen years later when I first mentioned the whole incident to Marty. He was twenty, a big, healthy, bearded, rural Oregonian in coveralls and boots. He let his mind muse over the prospects, then dismissed it with a laugh. It seemed so inconsequential to him, he didn't even thank me—which was exactly as it ought to have been.

So it was that I never exploited my son, or wrote pictures for my brother-in-law, or ever got higher up that ladder than writing a Western for an actor-producer named Rory Calhoun—an adaptation of a novel by Louis L'Amour, *The Last Stand at Apache Wells*. I put on my cowboy hat and went to work, simple enough until big Rory started bringing in different openings for the picture. Movie openings, it must be noted, were very special. All studio executives wanted to know, above all else, precisely how the picture would open. In fact, a clever writer could sell ideas for pictures merely by the artful depiction of an opening scene. Rory's suggested openings were all classic.

Dutifully, I took his pages and stuck them in, shifting what followed to suit his needs. As my work progressed, however, his subsequent openings became burdensome—especially when he suddenly included the discovery of a baby.

"A baby!" I protested.

"Yeah. And what a shocker that'll be!"

I allowed that this was so, but what did it have to do with the rest of the story?

"You're the writer," he said. "You figure that out."

It was all a farce. That New York writers such as I were writing cowboy-and-Indian pictures was itself a farce. That we knew precious little about the period seemed not to matter, for no one cared. Hollywood had re-created the American Indian for its cinematic needs and we were there to fill in the yarns. Countless films perpetuated the usual ethnic stereotypes, befouled the essence of Indian culture, violated history with lies and distortions. The film industry was proud of its censoring boards to protect the public from four-letter words, but no one was concerned over historical truth.

Who knew (or cared), for example, that it was the white man who originated scalping, that it was official policy in several colonies to pay bounties for Indian scalps, that the white man scalped Indians for profit as early as 1700!

For the American Indian—among other ethnic groups—the Hollywood "Dream Factory" had produced a nightmare.

I'd once heard of a movie in which an Indian actor was hired to translate the terms of a white man's treaty into the language of the Apaches, delivering this in a solemn end-of-the-picture scene. When the film was first screened at an Arizona reservation, however, the audience erupted in gales of hysterical laughter. The "translation," as it turned out, was the fabrication of the bitter Hollywood Indian telling his people that the treaty, the white man, the filmmakers, and especially this movie was a load of unmitigated bullshit!

To my brother-in-law's everlasting credit, he refused to appear for his Oscar award, sending an "Indian Princess" to register his protest that this insult might finally be stopped.

My swan song was a fitting conclusion to four inglorious years. I was doing another Western, this time at Warner Brothers, a picture about an Indian scout called *Yellowstone Kelly,* intended as a vehicle for John Wayne. At one point, I came to a snag in the scenario wherein Wayne, playing an old Indian scout, discovers the red-headed scalp of his best friend draped over the renegade Indian's horse. Since the climactic Wayne-Indian confrontation could not take place until the last reel, how would I get out of this scene? What, in effect, would an actor like Duke Wayne do in such a situation?

I had him dig a small grave, reverently bury the scalp, then top it with a small cross. My producer was wise enough to reject this, but offered no viable alternative. I immediately posed the problem to fellow writers around our regular luncheon table, creating an entertaining colloquy for several days, one solution being that Wayne should don the redheaded scalp himself and scare the evil enemy to death. In the end, however, my problems were solved by the presence of an old hand named Burt Kennedy who had written several pictures for Wayne and knew his style intimately.

Said Kennedy: "Duke would take one long, tender look at that scalp, then bash his big fist right into the Injun's horse's face!"

That's it, I thought, and everyone agreed.

I submitted this stirring solution as my second-act curtain, then went ahead to the simpler problems of the chase and final showdown. Three days later, however, my producer came to my office to tell me that Mr. Jack Warner himself wished to see me, and personally led me to the Old Man's office.

I was impressed, for this was hardly a routine experience for a lowly writer such as I. In fact, only once before had I met such a powerful figure, Harry Cohn of Columbia, who told me he was firing me: "You're a five-hundred-dollar-a-week writer, Asinof. A twenty-five-hundred-dollar-a-week writer does what I want him to do because he doesn't want to lose his job. You won't."

"Well, why don't you pay me twenty-five hundred dollars, Mr. Cohn?" I had dared to quip.

"Not you," he had said. "You still wouldn't do it."

Now I was working for Warner's, up to $850 a week, but far more compliant, I suspected.

"Asinof," said Jack Warner, fingering the pages of what I took to be my scenario, "you're a helluva writer, but I'm firing you."

"What!"

"This scene here with John Wayne and the horse. You got Wayne hitting a horse. Right in the kisser, you got it." He peered over his glasses and scowled at me, a look of utter revulsion. "I'm telling you that the Duke would never hit a horse. Never. To put a thing like that on the screen would be the damndest atrocity ever filmed. Any man who could write a thing like that oughta be blackballed right outa this town. One thing's for sure, you're through at this studio. Now get out!"

I left quickly enough, both amused and horrified. The producer apologized profusely for his helplessness, then concentrated on the problem of hiring my replacement—who turned out to be none other than Burt Kennedy.

So it was that *Yellowstone Kelly* was written and directed by Burt Kennedy, and starred not John Wayne, but Clint Walker, who also never hit a horse, except perhaps in self-defense.

When I finally left Hollywood in 1959, I had written six or eight such screenplays, another batch of treatments, a dozen or more television dramas, all of which were easily forgotten. To quote my agent at the time, Ingo Preminger: "Eliot, you should not be writing this nonsense. You should write marvelous books, then you can adapt them into marvelous screenplays and make a lot of marvelous money." Since my marriage had broken up (though I would not blame Hollywood for that), I returned to New York to try to become a writer again.

And naturally, my next book just happened to be about baseball.

21.

After my embattled history with the lawyers at Holt, Rinehart and Winston, when the Black Sox manuscript finally had the go-ahead, I felt like a starving wildcatter who had just struck oil.

I should have known better.

Howard Cady, too busy with administrative duties, assigned a young editor named John Blaylock to supervise the rewrites. Mine was to be John's very first book, and though he thought highly of my manuscript, he thought even more highly of his ability to improve on it.

"Eliot, Eliot," he would shake his head, "you have used the word *cantankerous* twice in this chapter!"

"Well, let's change one of them."

"I already have. In fact, I've rewritten both sentences. I really don't like that word at all."

And I would peer at my manuscript, blue lines slashing diagonally across whole paragraphs, new sentences scrawled between the lines. I was fully aware that I needed editing, but John issued no challenges, he merely rewrote, then confronted me with a fait accompli. It was done with such bravura, such absolute certainty, I could not help but be intimidated. After all, I'd spent five years atrophying in Lotus Land, hadn't I? For weeks, I sustained a growing sense of inadequacy as a craftsman, justifying the changes as his way of sparing me excessive criticism.

I wrestled with this. I would read his rewritten paragraphs and compare them with my originals, balancing one approach against the other. For the most part, I had written in short, staccato sentences in the belief that it would keep the action moving fluidly through my vast, disparate cast of characters. Where I had written: "The Little Champ, Abe Attell, had a fine box seat behind third base. The hot sun beat down on his taut little body, but never disturbed his impeccably tailored clothes. He could tell you: he'd done his sweating in the ring for over a dozen years"; Blaylock had rewritten it into one sentence: "In his impeccably tailored clothes, the Little Champ, Abe Attell, sat in an excellent box seat behind third base, and though the hot sun engulfed his taut little body, his years in the ring had rendered it impervious to such minor irritants."

Though I alone would decide what appeared on the printed page, it gave me small surcease. Every workday became a torment, a return to do battle with his overly determined blue pencil. Then, one Monday morning, I entered his office and saw the freshly typed pages in front of him—his typewriter, not mine—with the familiar names of Rothstein, Attell, et al.

"Eliot, I'm sure you'll see what I mean when you read this . . ." he began, and suddenly I went berserk. Empowered by a dramatic surge of adrenaline, I grabbed the top lid of his desk by its undersurface and lifted it, dumping the entire manuscript on his lap like a dump truck evacuating garbage.

Poor John. He cried out in fear as the avalanche of paper all but buried him. His secretary came rushing in, aghast at the sight of him sprawled on the floor, his chair having rolled a few feet away before it, too, toppled over. In time, we righted the desk and its papers. Blaylock regained his poise and I, my self-control. Let it be said that I never read any more freshly typed pages. Indeed, he completely reappraised my capacity to write, seldom suggesting any changes unless I actively solicited them.

So it was that the process ended in a friendly fashion with the restoration of my manuscript to its original style. To his credit, Blaylock supplied a workable title, *Eight Men Out,* and I quickly agreed it was the best of the lot.

Six months later, in the early summer of 1963, there were five thousand finished books. The merchandise was finally available.

The real action was about to begin.

Every season, a very few books are treated as publishing successes long before their release. Lucrative paperback-reprint deals are made, book clubs pay large sums for exclusivity, Hollywood studios buy the rights for motion pictures, a leading national magazine publishes a condensation. Huge first printings assure that a flood of copies overwhelm the book buyer in every major bookstore in America. Even before the book is reviewed, advertisements appear in leading cities to proclaim a major event in publishing history.

None of this happened with *Eight Men Out.*

But something else did.

It began on the date of publication, when both *The New York Times* and the *Herald Tribune* gave the book a rousing send-off, while early that very morning, I appeared on NBC's "Today Show" in a fine twenty-five-minute interview with Hugh Downs and Jack Lascoulie, both of whom had actually read the book. By noon, I was informed that highly laudatory reviews dominated the front pages of Sunday supplements in Los Angeles, San Francisco, and Chicago, an almost unprecedented occurrence. On subsequent days, dozens more reviews filtered in from all over the country in a torrent of accolades.

It was marvelous. All those goodies happened so unexpectedly, one after another in what appeared to be a never-ending flow. I was repeatedly told that this would certainly build to a best seller, the magic phrase that suggests success, money, fame, security. As every writer knows, one best seller almost automatically creates a market for another. From my $2,500 advance, no doubt my royalties would leap to $50,000 or more.

So it was that I was sent on the author's tour to publicize the book. I returned to Chicago basking in a glow of triumph. Studs Terkel interviewed me for his FM radio show, reading passages from my book as though it were *War and Peace.* Robert Cromie had me on his nationally syndicated television show "Book Beat," wherein he advised his viewers that I had made the Black Sox Scandal a memorable piece of social history. In another sop to my ego I sat in the huge Krocks-Brentano Bookstore for an hour, autographing hundreds of books in towering stacks while at least a dozen purchases were made in my presence.

Then, as though the gods wanted to crush any false hopes I might be generating, came a succession of warnings, one after another—a clutter of trivia, but nonetheless telling.

First of all there was the "Kup Show," another syndicated sit-around that went on for several hours, on this day with a mixed bag of distinguished guests, such as Adlai Stevenson, General S. L. A. Marshall, actresses Jeanne Crain and Merle Oberon, novelist Herbert Kubly, and finally, myself. Irv Kupcinet, the host, an ex–football star from the Big Ten, was a burly, friendly man with an easy way about him, especially with show folk. He knew all about what Jeanne Crain and Merle Oberon were promoting in Chicago (a play and a motion picture), but when it came to the writers, he resorted to what may well be the worst interview line ever delivered: "Tell us what your book is about, Mr. Kubly."

In that instant, Kubly winced, then, conscious that the camera must have pinpointed it, broke into a stammering sweat. He simply did not know where to begin. Like the others, I was overcome with embarrassment. Then, touched by a sudden surge of courage, I volunteered as a colleague to describe Kubly's theme and the thrust of his main characters, having taken the trouble to read much of it on the previous evening. In this way, I initiated a discussion of sorts, precisely what the host should have done.

There are no statistics on such matters, but I doubt that either Kubly or Asinof sold any books as a result of that show. I am inclined to believe that the beautiful ladies Crain and Oberon fared infinitely better. Still, as publicity-oriented people are quick to explain, this sort of promotion is supposed to be cumulative, a steady building of your name and the title. I came to question any such accumulation, my theory being that the author had no more status with the audience than he had with the show's host.

With my new bravado (enhanced by boredom) I put this alleged theory to the test on the following day—another radio talk show known as "Luncheon with Sig." I presented myself to the host, Sig Sakowitz, at the appointed hour and was told that I'd be first—which, of course, was fine with me. I sat at his table and awaited the call to action. It began as follows:

"Good afternoon, ladies and gents, this is Sig Sakowitz, and we've got a splendid group of celebrities with us today. Chuck Connors, the Rifleman on TV; that glittering movie star Jeanne Crain; the magnificent Merle Oberon; and more, many more. First off, though, I take great pleasure in introducing a distinguished writer from New York . . ." Here, Sig fumbled with his papers, looking for my distinguished name, and failing to find it, quite naturally turned the matter over to me. "Tell us who you are," he said.

It was more than I could handle. Suddenly possessed by the devil himself, I offered what I assumed they wanted to hear: "Irwin Shaw," I said.

Sig blanched, stared at me under a wave of curiosity.

"Ha ha," he said. "We're joking. Come on, now. Everyone wants to know," and he kept fumbling with those papers.

"Irving Wallace."

Another ha ha, more paper fumbling, and this time he glared at me, his teeth gnashing with menace. (After all, this was radio, not television.)

"A regular jokester," he smiled into the mike. Then, more

politely, "I assure you sir, everyone *really* wants to know . . ."

"Norman Mailer." Then, quickly, "No, Harold Robbins."

Lucky for old Sig, his assistant came running to the rescue, the program list in hand, furiously pointing to my name at its top.

"Ladies and gentlemen, his name is Eliot Asinof, and he's written an absolutely marvelous book called *Eight Men Out.*"

He took a beat, presumably to settle me down.

Then, with great seriousness, "Tell us what your book is about, Eliot . . ."

I simply could not reply. Having planned no smart-ass ploy, I found myself staggered by my own idiotic derring-do. Having gotten my feet wet, then, I could hardly be blamed for going in up to my knees.

Besides, I thought, who could possibly care?

"Well, it's a book about eight old friends who graduated from college twenty years ago, and now they were together in a reunion for the first time . . ." I then proceeded to deliver a totally scatterbrained version of Mary McCarthy's recently published novel *The Group.* Sig seemed pleased, if only because I appeared to be making more sense than anything I'd said previously. Besides, it was literate enough to fill three or four minutes without dead air.

"What a fascinating book it is!" he chirped, then thanked me profusely for joining him.

A moment later, I rejoined a group of friends seated at a rear table, none of whom had been able to hear a word of it.

"How'd it go?" they asked.

"I'll be anxious to find out," I replied.

The answer was an absolute zero. To my knowledge the show went totally without responsive listeners. Certainly, none called in to protest or even comment. What I had dared to do made no more sense than spitting into the wind. My one small victory came ten years later, when Bob Cromie, in his keynote speech at the National Book Awards in New York, used this incident as an illustration of the touring author's plight.

Sig Sakowitz's press releases continue to appear regularly in my mailbox.

I left Chicago for points west, somewhat soured toward publicity devices but as enthusiastic as ever about the prospects for my book. By the time I reached Los Angeles, however, I was ready for the wipeout.

On my first day there, I was hit by one of those cutting ironies that can bleed an author to a lingering death. Instructed by the Holt publicity department to appear at the Pickwick Bookstore on Hollywood Boulevard—the largest bookstore in all of Greater Los Angeles—for another autograph-signing binge, I presented myself to Lloyd Harkimer, the manager, whom I knew from earlier years as a resident. He greeted my arrival with sardonic laughter.

"Autograph books? We have none. There's not a single copy of your book in Los Angeles!"

I sank in confusion as he spilled out the sordid details, gratified that someone was obviously telling me the whole gory truth—as much a rarity in the publishing business as anywhere in Hollywood. As Lloyd told it, only a small part of his order for books had arrived. And why had he not been informed that I was to appear on the "Today Show," especially as a major personality on its most prominent time slot, always a big seller of books in that city (as elsewhere)? That, plus the remarkable front-page review in the Sunday *Los Angeles Times*, built up an instant demand for *Eight Men Out*, and Pickwick sold out the dozen or so copies available in less than an hour after the store had opened. His desperate attempt at getting more books in stock had failed since the West Coast jobber himself had only a short supply.

"Eliot," he sighed, "I could have sold over five hundred copies in this store alone!"

It was the same in other leading bookstores in Beverly Hills, and, I would learn, in San Francisco as well. Considerably miffed, I canceled scheduled appearances on local television interview shows, unwilling to waste time selling a book that could not be bought.

How to explain such a mind-boggling bungle? It was as if a nation's army was conscripted, outfitted, trained, convoyed overseas, then finally transferred to the front—only to discover someone had forgotten to ship the ammunition.

But, then, I had never done well in Los Angeles, had I?

22.

Then, in the midst of my frustration, a moment of magic: my new agent called with the extraordinary news that Twentieth Century-Fox wanted to buy my book.

"No kidding!" I cried out.

"No kidding."

"How much?"

"I think we can get a hundred thousand."

"Jesus . . ." I gasped.

That afternoon, we drove over to Fox and the office of producer Aaron Rosenberg. It was true. He really wanted to buy the book.

"I see this as the first sports picture ever made that will have real meaning," Aaron said. "Like *The Grapes of Wrath* was a Western."

"Fine," I said.

Richard Zanuck, son of Darryl, was the studio executive behind it. I sat there glowing, barely able to keep from bursting into laughter at every flattering word, titillating myself with the prospect of $100,000 and the zillion more that such a film would bring to my book.

"I want you to meet my writer, Sidney Boehm," Aaron was saying. "He has some great ideas on how to deal with the story."

Sure enough, Sidney appeared from his office upstairs, a distinguished screenwriter with a long list of credits.

"Your book is marvelous, Eliot. It gives us a chance to say

something. I see this as the first sports picture to have meaning, like *The Grapes of Wrath* was a Western."

I nodded, wondering if he had originated the line or Aaron.

"I seldom get my hands on work as rich as this," he went on. "So many wonderful characters. So much to think about. It's a never-ending feast . . ."

"Yeah . . . those guys were something, all right," I agreed.

It went on like that for a dozen minutes, as lovey-dovey as any honeymoon ever made in heaven.

"Tell Eliot how you see the opening, Sidney," Aaron said.

Sidney nodded, rearranged himself in his chair, leaned forward with clenched fist pounding an open palm. Out of sheer nervous anticipation, I held my breath, nodding slowly in encouragement.

"I see it opening in a nightclub," he began. "You know, garish, noisy, the sort of place where the Big Boys go to be seen. We see Arnold Rothstein with a beautiful doll in a low-cut dress. He points to the door and says to her: 'See that big hunk of man? That's Chick Gandil, the baseball player, and I want you to suck his cock,' or, you know, words to that effect. Rothstein calls Gandil over and buys him a drink while the babe goes to work on him, you know, some wet-eyed looks, a hand on his knee. Then she gets up to join the band— she's a singer, see—and belts out a number especially for Gandil. That way we get in a little music of the period while we move the story along. You follow?"

As we used to say in the army, I didn't know whether to piss or go blind. What happened was, I became dizzy. A slight case of shock, no doubt. I'd gone from suppressed laughter to the brink of tears in a matter of seconds.

Here, my agent cut in with appropriate compliments. "Sidney, you are one of Hollywood's great storytellers," then rose to declare that time was pressing him, he had another appointment over at Metro. He assured Aaron (and Sidney) that I would be available for whatever "technical advice" they might need once the contracts had been signed. He then drew Aaron into a corner for what I assumed to be a brief agreement on terms, and we left.

157

"Well, I think it'll be eighty thou, Eliot," he said when we got into his Lincoln Continental.

"Fine!" I said, though the word came out sounding like an obscenity.

"Don't worry about the screenplay," he chuckled, trying to make light of my rancor. "They always sound a lot worse than they read . . ."

It had been my experience that the opposite was true, that screenplays generally start from a reasonably dramatic concept, then shrivel into dried-up clichés.

"Well, *The Grapes of Wrath* was a helluva movie," I said, making jokes at my anguish. He laughed, though not very comfortably. I let the memory of that opening scene fester until, like an adolescent fool, I had to make a comment: "Christ, what shit!"

"Relax," he said, and patted my knee. "Sidney Boehm is a first-rate screenwriter. I'd be proud to have him for a client—just as I'm proud to have you."

When an agent speaks, the words have only one function: make the sale. That Gandil was going to get his cock sucked, or that other abominations were going to be inflicted on my book, was of no concern to him. I struggled to contain my petulance, fully aware that my mood would build to fresh layers of impotence as I contemplated my options. I needed to talk this over with someone, but not with this man. Indeed, the thought that I was facing such problems in the company of an agent only compounded my frustrations. What the hell, he had $8,000 on the come, no doubt a down payment on next year's Continental. I roiled at that one. I had gotten no more than $2,500 for writing the book, and here was a man who was going to get $8,000 for merely driving me to the studio and back. What's more, that kind of money was his right, built into the system as immutably as death and taxes. To struggling writers, agents seemed as much like tycoons as studio heads. They all drove these incredible cars, lived in sumptuous homes, socialized with the stars. They didn't even have to pay for the dozen copies of my book they requested in anticipation of its movie sale; the author did. As my agent, this man was going to make $8,000 for spending less time and effort than it took me to get into Happy Felsch's parlor. More than likely, Aaron Rosenberg would buy *him* a bottle of Chivas Regal for bringing my book to him.

Years before, when I'd first come to Hollywood, I was taken to a party at the beautiful home of a successful agent named Paul Kohner. At one point during the evening, I stood on his patio by the blue-lit swimming pool looking out at the twinkling lights of Beverly Hills in the valley below. Kohner sidled up beside me, reading my envy, no doubt.

"Just remember, Eliot," he said in his continental accent, "all this comes from the ten percent, not the ninety."

On this afternoon, eight years after that party, I was certainly not in rebellion against the system. The truth was, I was pleased to be in this man's Continental (I don't believe I'd ever ridden in one before), and perfectly agreeable to accepting the 90 percent. My distress was over the perceptions, not the percentages. Grotesque images were floating across my mind as though on that silver screen itself, a series of distorted gargoyles named Gandil, Jackson, Cicotte, Weaver making jerks of themselves.

"Why can't you arrange it so that I write the script?" I offered.

"Sorry. Aaron made that clear from the beginning. He likes to work with Sidney."

Yes, he'd told me that. But I struggled on. "I was hoping that maybe I could at least collaborate with him . . ."

"Eliot . . ." He began to clear his throat in the patronizing manner of one about to deliver a lecture. "What you have to accept is that a sale is what the word means: a sale. When you sell, you relinquish all rights. You don't have script approval. Oh, there are cases where important novelists were given concessions, this director, that actor, but the studios don't cotton to that, so forget it."

Then, anticipating my only option, he was confident enough to rub my nose in it: "Of course, no one can force an author to sell his book . . ."

The sonovabitch was taunting me. Of the three thousand or so American writers, I'd heard of only *one* who had taken such a stalwart position. One pure artistic soul out of three thousand. He was J. D. Salinger, whose *Catcher in the Rye* was simply not for sale to the motion-picture industry.

"Well, I'll think it over," I said, at least making a stab at defiance.

He let that hang in the air for a moment, and when he returned to action, he spoke with a whole new tone.

"I'll tell you something, Eliot. I have to admire you. I seldom get a writer who doesn't jump for the money. You really care about your book. I saw the way you almost jumped out of your shoes. You want to know something? If you decided against the sale, I wouldn't blame you at all. In fact, I'd have nothing but respect for you." Then patting my knee again: "I want you to know that."

"Thanks," I said.

A great little speech, all right. One of the Agents' Commandments: "Thou shalt always tell a client what he wants to hear." My honor thus placated, I could more readily rationalize any compromises. Indeed, I could feel the resistance oozing out of me.

So we drove the rest of the way in silence, through those glittering broad streets of Beverly Hills lined with towering palms and magnificent homes, in the rear of which I imagined beautiful nude women lolling beside sparkling swimming pools. He pushed a button, and the car was filled with music, while I suffered through a crazy daydream of scampering up one of those trees just to see if such delicious treats were visible from the summit. We turned into Sunset Boulevard, hardly a mile from his office, when the music suddenly stopped for a special newscast.

Very special, as it turned out. In fact, it was absolutely devastating—and unbelievable.

"Paul Caruso, attorney for Walter 'Dutch' Ruether, former pitcher for the Cincinnati Reds, announced the initiation of a lawsuit against publisher Holt, Rinehart and Winston of a book entitled *Eight Men Out: The Black Sox and the 1919 World Series,* and its author, Eliot Asinof. Currently a scout for the San Francisco Giants, Ruether is demanding one million dollars for defamation of character destructive to his reputation, plus another one million dollars punitive damages . . ."

We had hardly gotten back to the agent's office when it became clear that Zanuck himself had heard the news.

"Well, that does it," the agent sighed. "Any threat of litigation will always kill a deal . . ."

My head was spinning with speculation about what I had written about Ruether, but the agent didn't even ask. There was a copy of my book on his shelf and I immediately went for it. Ruether had been a winner and a hero to Cincinnati. I could find only one possible pejorative paragraph—a reference to Ring Lardner, no less:

> [Ring] came into the room laughing, a clear sign he had uncovered some delicate vignette that piqued his misanthropic nature. In this case, it involved the Cincinnati pitcher, "Dutch" Ruether, scheduled to start on the morrow. Lardner had seen him drinking heavily just a few minutes before. Fullerton immediately called Pat Moran, Reds manager, to report this. Moran thanked him and told him of a plot he'd heard about: a few Chicago gamblers were trying to get his whole pitching staff drunk. Ruether, who was a serious drinker, had somehow eluded Moran's scouts.

"Two million dollars for *that!*"

"It's not the two mill, Eliot," the agent was quick to explain. "It's the eighty thou."

The Mummy's Curse. Right?

Or, as they say: "That's show business!"

I've never heard anything that said it better.

As far as Walter "Dutch" Ruether's claims were concerned, one might think that there was really nothing to worry about. The absurdity was evident in the verbiage alone, and I would beseech the reader to feast on the following legal gobbledygook:

4	That by the use and publication of said words and language,
5	used and published by the defendants as aforesaid, they, and
6	each of them, intended to charge and assert, and to be
7	understood as charging and asserting, and by the readers of
8	said book were, in fact, understood as charging and asserting,
9	that this plaintiff, in violation of his trust as an employee of the
10	Cincinnati baseball team, was heavily drinking the day before
11	he was to pitch the opening game of the World Series, and was
12	an unloyal, irresponsible and untrustworthy member of the
13	team; that this plaintiff was an alcoholic, and that the
14	consumption of alcohol was a primary interest and weakness
15	of plaintiff, and that plaintiff had an addiction to the excessive
16	use of liquor, and had resourcefully and intentionally promoted
17	this excessive use; that this plaintiff, in violation of his trust
18	and confidence as a member of the Cincinnati baseball club,
19	organized baseball, and the American sports public, had made
20	himself accessible to dishonest and corrupt gamblers who
21	intended to fix the World Series, and that he intentionally made
22	himself available to their corrupt interests; that this plaintiff
23	was amenable to a proposition that involved fixing of the World
24	Series, and that this plaintiff was not adverse to a plot that
25	involved the fixing of the World Series, and that this plaintiff
26	was considered not to be adverse to such a plot by corrupt and
27	dishonest gamblers who had such an intention, and that
28	plaintiff's reputation was such that he would not be adverse to
29	such a corrupt and dishonest plan; that this plaintiff, in
30	disregard of the interests of his teammates, his employers, and
31	the American public, intentionally let himself become the dupe
32	in the machinations of corrupt gamblers; and that this
33	plaintiff consorted and associated with gamblers who intended
34	to fix the World Series.

PAUL CARUSO
ATTORNEY AT LAW
BEVERLY HILLS, CALIF.

Of course, several weeks later, there was another action, from northern California, where Arnold "Chick" Gandil was putting in his own oar: another $2,000,000 lawsuit that claimed I'd done things to him that were even worse.

I wasn't worried about such matters. There was no way in which either of these claims could hold up, much less even get to court. Besides, aren't such publicized lawsuits a boon for book sales?

My publishers, however, had a different view of it. Their neck was in a double noose, it did not matter how loosely drawn. On advice of counsel, they chose not to exploit the publicity out of fear of exacerbating the problem. They even stopped all subsequent advertisements. And to compound the defeat, the potential for a paperback-reprint deal appeared to be quickly squashed.

Once again, then, it was the Time of the Lawyers. As preposterous as the claims might be, they still had to be defended. Lawyers, I would quickly learn, had a polite and easy way with each other, and they took time to work out their problems, lots of time, for which they billed a handsome hourly fee. I assumed that Mr. Caruso in Los Angeles had taken the Ruether case on a contingency basis, as had Gandil's lawyer. I also assumed that they never believed they could win in court, but would merely create a harassment, seeking to induce the wealthy publisher to agree to an out-of-court settlement.

And needless to say, I was adamantly against any such thing, taking note of that standard clause in my contract wherein the author is held responsible for half of the legal expenses resulting from the contents of his work. From where I sat, I had neither libeled nor defamed anyone. I had documented everything. And when I met with the publisher's lawyers in New York (presumably the same gentlemen who had advised against publishing the year before), I made this position clear. Again, I presented my sources—two large corrugated boxes of papers and books—agreeing to do everything I could to assist them in our mutual defense. Apparently, however, the trouble lay in a unique California law that applied less to libel than to invasion of privacy, wherein one cannot write of a person's former malfeasances when that person is currently living a life of rectitude. It mattered less that I had told the truth than that I might have damaged their reputations.

"Of course," the attorneys were quick to add, "it is vitally important to our defense that you did tell the truth. Any judge would have to be responsive to that."

They were primarily concerned about the Ruether case, in spite of the fact that Gandil's claim might seem considerably stronger, the reasons being that Paul Caruso was a lawyer of considerable clout, and that Los Angeles courts were more inclined to adjudicate this sort of case than the courts of San Francisco. Further, Gandil was not likely to pursue the action in San Francisco unless Ruether was successful in L.A.

"Then, what can we do?" came my plaintive query.

"Not much, at this point," came the reply, "unless we can dissuade Ruether from pursuing this."

I would certainly try, I said. The best I could come up with was a call to Bill Veeck, then owner of the Cleveland Indians.

"Two mill! You ought to be proud, Eliot. I don't know any writers who get sued for that kind of dough."

"How well do you know Ruether?" I asked.

"Very well. He used to work for me."

"Jesus, Bill. He's killing me. I even had a movie deal!"

"What do you want *me* to do?"

"Can you talk to him? Tell him he's nuts or something. I mean, all I did was quote Ring Lardner saying he was downing a few too many . . ."

"The Dutchman likes the sauce, all right," he agreed.

But Veeck was skeptical. "I don't know, El. He always gets eager when he smells a dollar."

"Bill, we've *got* to get him to quit."

He promised to try, and I knew he would. He was a man of many parts, not the least of which was his affection for books and writers.

Weeks later, at 4:00 A.M., my phone rang. In a semistupor, I scrambled out of bed to answer it.

"Yes . . . ?"

"Eliot, Eliot, how are you?" It was Veeck's laughing, throaty voice.

"Oh, hi." I heard lots of talk in the background, the sounds of party noises. "Hey, Bill, where are you?"

"Minneapolis." Then I remembered. Big doings on the eve of the 1963 World Series. "Got a helluva bash going on in my room," he said. "And guess who's here?"

"Ruether," I said, "Dutch Ruether."

Veeck laughed. "Right."

Beat.

Then, anxiously, "Well, did you talk him out of it?" I asked. "Did you?"

"How can I, El . . . *he's too damn drunk!*"

More background laughter, and Veeck, that marvelous sonovabitch, was laughing too.

And that was the end of that.

Meanwhile, as Gandil must have waited in the wings, Ruether's lawsuit against the book dragged on, its legal papers and letters continuing to expand the files in various law offices from Los Angeles to New York. I saw none of them and cared less. During this time, I was advised by attorneys not to go to California lest papers be served on me there, thereby placing me, my savings, my future earnings, in jeopardy. Nonetheless, I went, repeatedly, for my son lived there, and the principal source of my income was writing for television films. I would, however, seek some small measure of satisfaction at the Los Angeles airport by writing "Ha ha, Eliot Asinof" on a postcard to Paul Caruso just before boarding.

Then, in the spring of 1966, two and a half years after that jarring radio report in my agent's Continental, the case was finally dismissed by a California court.

Shortly thereafter, I received a letter from my publisher advising me that their legal expenses in defense of this action came to $5,343.66, half of which I was liable for according to contract.

"This is upsetting but unavoidable," the letter concluded.

To me, the figures were staggering. My guess was that I had spent at least as much time working on the defense as the attorneys had, yet they were getting paid more money for this case than I had made on the book itself! The whole thing was ludicrous. Any lawyer can file a hundred such complaints, spraying them out like buckshot in hopes that one will net a substantial settlement—for which he will receive a mammoth share. It matters little that his client's complaint is a feeble one; his strength lies in the power of harassment, for the defendant must hire an attorney to defend a no-win situation. The longer the matter can be stretched, the greater the chance for a compromise settlement—at which *both* lawyers become beneficiaries. It is a system devised by lawyers, and, most certainly, perpetuated by them.

Little did I know that ten years later I would have to face the full brunt of this sort of thing alone.

Upsetting but unavoidable, indeed.

For reasons of my sanity as well as my finances, and (to crown the irony) *on advice of counsel,* I chose to ignore the publisher's letter. For reasons of compassion and God knows what else, the publishers did not pursue it.

24.

As for *Eight Men Out,* after total sales of 9,600 copies, it gradually drifted out of print. The few copies lingering in bookstores here and there became exceedingly hard to find. A collector's item, it was flatteringly called. For all intents and purposes, the book was dead.

My total earnings had come to $4,725.23.

Karl Marx once wrote that a writer should not live and write to make money, he should live and make money to write.

I was having difficulty with either alternative.

Above all, I wanted to keep the book alive, preferably with a paperback edition that would reach a mass market. Eventually, I found acceptance at Ace Books, of Charter Communications, a reprint house that featured gothic novels and science fiction. They even advanced me $1,000.

As a result, a year later, *Eight Men Out* was still alive (though not particularly well) and living in assorted paperback stands throughout the country. After printing a hundred thousand, sixty thousand copies were sold, the remaining forty thousand languishing in warehouses.

It was something of a treat, then, when Mel Sokolow, an executive at Warner Paperback Library, told me of his admiration for my book and his desire to put it on their list, if only they could get hold of the rights.

Marvelous, I thought. Warner's was a new star in the reprint galaxy and would do a far better job than Ace in distributing it. I told Mel I would get the rights back myself, immediately proceeding to do so—at the cost of the same $1,000 Ace had paid for it. Fair enough, I thought; would I not get many times that at Warner's? I mailed Charter Communications a check for which I was given a covering letter assuring me of the destruction of the forty thousand copies still in print. I then marched over to the Warner offices, delivering a hardcover copy of *Eight Men Out* together with my huge portfolio of all those glowing reviews.

"Fine," Sokolow said, and promised to call me shortly.

A month or so later, it was I who called him.

"What's going on?" I asked.

"I'm sorry," he replied hurriedly (he was in the middle of a meeting), "but we're going to pass on it."

"But you can't!" I protested.

"It's not a comment on your wonderful book, El . . . It's just that the top guys here don't think it will sell."

The Curse again. Max Baer, the heavyweight fighter, used to laugh when he got hit in a magnificent show of defiance, or so I read it. As for me, I laughed out of helplessness.

It is said that failure has a tendency to feed on itself, the flip side of that other adage, "Money comes to money." The sense of it leaks out, nothing absolute or definitive, just a whiff here and there, and it's enough to rattle a man's confidence. It begins to show in his eyes, emitting that "rancid smell of defeat," as Mickey Spillane once put it.

I was ruminating on that late one night while driving along the Palisades Parkway in New Jersey when I spotted the spinning party hat of a patrol car in my rear-view mirror. Though I was definitely not speeding, there was no doubt that I was the target. I pulled over and prepared myself for whatever defeat was in store for me.

"Evening . . ." the policeman said.

"Evening."

"You got a busted taillight."

"Oh?" I got out and checked. It was broken, all right. The entire right rear was quite badly mauled, and not of particularly recent vintage. The car was about eight years old and showed more than the usual urban signs of age. I had never been a car buff—a fact that was clearly apparent at the moment. However guilty I appeared to be, it suddenly became terribly important that I beat this rap, for I needed a turning point, a victory to take to bed with me, and I went at it with all the guile I could generate.

"Officer, that must have happened this afternoon. I know, that's no excuse, but I live in the city, and this car lives in the streets. I mean, there's just no way to prevent this sort of thing."

He paid no attention to what I was saying, just stood there staring, first at the car, then at my license and registration. I took the measure of his equivocation and poured on another layer of defense.

"I'm a man who respects the law, officer. If you look at my license, you'll see there's not a single moving offense listed there. I'm a very careful driver. I know, this is something else, but I repeat, I couldn't help it. I can assure you, I'll get it fixed first thing tomorrow . . ."

He was walking around the car, checking the other lights, even the tires. I watched him, waiting for some sign as to which way he might go.

"What's your line of work, mister?" he asked, still holding the papers.

I always mistrusted that question, for it suggested all sorts of hidden meanings. After all, what conceivable connection did a man's profession have to a busted taillight? From my point of view, it posed the counterquestions: Was one line of work more or less susceptible to a summons than another? If so, which? I had heard that the police will give a lawyer the benefit of the doubt, presumably more out of wariness than sympathy. So I'd tried that once, actually telling an officer that I was an attorney, and he immediately wrote out the summons.

"I'm a writer," I said, somewhat tentatively, I suspect.

"A writer?" He seemed exceptionally curious. "What kind of writer?"

"Books, articles, television plays . . ."

He looked at me with a touch of incredulity, then shook his head as he took one last look at my car.

"Mister," he said, "you must be one *lousy* writer to be driving a heap like this!"

Then he handed back my license and left without another word.

25.

It took the scandal at Watergate in 1972 to bring on the revival of *Eight Men Out*. As that insidious story leaked out, I began to hear references to the Black Sox Scandal and the 1919 World Series. One scandal recapitulating another. Two portraits of hypocrisy at work, one hand swearing eternal fealty to truth and the pursuit of honor, while the other shoveled dirt to conceal its evil doings.

By 1974, I began hearing fresh inquiries about movie rights from the new breed of filmmakers that pervaded New York. There were literally hundreds of them, many with completed films throbbing in cans, begging for release on theatrical screens, and a few of them came eagerly to my door.

"It's time to make this picture!" they said, and I agreed.

"What sort of money are you thinking about?" I asked.

"Money? We don't have money. We want to tie up the property so we can work on it. The screenplay will take us six months or so . . ."

Eventually, there was an offer, an option of $2,500 to bind the rights for two years, from a production company owned by Douglas Schmidt. I was fully aware that this was hardly a substantial sum, but in light of the dozen barren years that preceded it, I found myself warmed by the prospects. For merely an option I was being paid as much as the publisher had paid me for writing the book.

Besides, I liked Schmidt. His insight and enthusiasm lent dignity to the project. And though he did not have the resources to hire me as screenwriter, his own writing colleagues seemed solidly in tune with the thrust of my book.

So we signed an agreement in May 1974, and therein lay the source of the great controversies to come.

What pleased me most at the time was that *Eight Men Out* was alive once again. What I did not foresee was the extraordinary extent to which this was so. No sooner had I agreed to put the book in Schmidt's hands for two years than the phone began to ring from the other coast. Nor were these calls from neophytes, however spirited and high-minded. The old pros were seeking me out again. Not surprisingly, I suppose, among the first was Aaron Rosenberg (of Twentieth Century-Fox) himself.

"After all these years, Eliot, I'm still after your book."

"Must be a record," I said.

He stopped laughing when I told him my book was not available.

There were calls from Mike Green of Twentieth Century-Fox, and Jack Haley, Jr., head of its television department; several independent producers in association with United Artists and Warner Brothers; producer-director Robert Altman (whose father had lost a bundle on the 1919 Series) was interested. Over the next six months, I received over a dozen more inquiries, but my eggs were resting in Doug Schmidt's basket. I could only wait and see if they would hatch.

Then, late in the winter of 1975, there was that fateful call from David Susskind:

"Eliot . . ." he had said cheerfully, with barely a moment of small talk, "I want to buy *Eight Men Out.*"

BOOK THREE

"Cheshire-Puss," she began . . . "Would you tell me, please, which way I ought to go from here?"

"In that direction," the Cat said, waving its right paw round, "lives a Hatter: and in that direction," waving the other paw, "lives a March Hare. Visit either you like: they're both mad."

"But I don't want to go among mad people," Alice remarked.

"Oh, you can't help that," said the Cat: "we're all mad here. I'm mad. You're mad."

"How do you know I'm mad?" said Alice.

"You must be," said the Cat, "or you wouldn't have come here."

26.

Ed Costikyan smiled as I finished, shaking his head in amusement while reviewing the notes he had taken.

"What's so funny?" I asked. Having poured out my guts for over an hour, I felt I had a right to know.

"I was just remembering the vicious way you hit a golf ball . . ."

"What about it?" I asked.

"Like it was Susskind's head," he said.

He fingered through the COMPLAINT, scanning the pages until he reached the relevant paragraphs.

Then he read aloud:

" 'Upon information and belief, Asinof, with full knowledge of the Agreement and the subsequent dealings with NBC and TA concerning the Script, did willfully and intentionally induce NBC not to exercise the option in the Agreement' . . . blah blah blah . . . 'by maliciously threatening to sue NBC . . .' "

He stopped there, looking up at me. "Did you threaten to sue?"

"Quite the contrary," I replied. "As I told you, when Bill Storke of NBC said I had the right to sue, I very specifically noted that I had no intention to. I told him that I was not the litigious type."

Costikyan nodded, then read on. Again he stopped, this time at paragraph ten.

" 'Upon information and belief, Asinof falsely and maliciously slandered and defamed TA by stating to officers of NBC and the International Business Machines Corp., the proposed sponsor of the Special, that the script unlawfully "infringed" Asinof's copyrighted book . . .' "

He was looking at me again.

"Did you claim infringement of copyright?" he asked.

"I don't even know what it means."

"That the script uses the material in your book without the rights to do so."

"Again, the truth is exactly the opposite: I claimed the script was inaccurate precisely because it did not."

Again, he returned to the COMPLAINT, reading the last two pages rapidly, pausing briefly at the end to tally up the size of damages.

"One million, seven hundred fifty thousand," he said.

"Yeah, I finally made the Big Leagues."

"Well, it's not much of a case," he admitted.

"I'm not worried about losing, Ed. What bothers me is the cost of defending."

He nodded, giving it thought. "There's a compromise solution here somewhere. It all depends on what Susskind wants out of this. We'll just have to find out what it is."

"Suppose he's just angry," I speculated. "Suppose he just wants to punish me . . ."

He shrugged. "I always proceed on the assumption of compromise. For your purposes, the sooner the better. These things become expensive after a while."

"And if not?"

He shook his head at the prospect of bad news. "You have to stand trial."

"And how much would that cost me?"

"A bundle."

"How big a bundle?" I braced myself.

"It could go to twenty or twenty-five thousand dollars." Then, quietly, "Maybe more."

The reappearance of that figure seemed terribly ominous, a flip-flop from plus $25,000 to minus $25,000 in hardly more than the winking of a lawyer's eye.

It gives one pause.

Weeks before, when I'd first received the COMPLAINT, I'd staggered under the threat of the costly solutions during a visit to Steve Weinrib, my lawyer friend.

Of course, he, too, had broken out laughing.

"You couldn't take the money, could you?" he'd chided me.

"Get me out of this," I'd pleaded.

"All I can do is file a denial."

"What about a countersuit?" I asked. "Isn't that a routine tactic under these circumstances?"

Presumably, it would be based on the damages Susskind had done *me*, namely his attacks on my equity vis-à-vis my option agreement with Doug Schmidt, that preposterous claim that TA owned all rights to my book since the 1960 agreement.

"Well, it's a possibility," he said. "But you've got to consider . . . if Susskind is really mad at you, he might countersue your countersuit."

"How?" I asked.

"By claiming that *Eight Men Out* and all its royalties belonged to TA, starting with that research outline you wrote."

"But no one has it. How could he claim he owned the book based on research he doesn't have?"

"He can claim anything he wants to claim! Besides, how can you be so sure he doesn't have it?"

I didn't even want to think in such terms. To condition a defense out of fear that I never owned the book I'd written was too absurd. From where a lawyer sat, however, it was definitely a consideration. One could picture Susskind sitting with *his* attorneys in a comparable strategy meeting, all that high-priced, highly trained talent applying itself to this ruse or that.

"Besides . . ." Steve advised me, "I'm not a trial lawyer. This firm doesn't take cases to trial."

"Steve . . ." I began speculating with desperate alternatives. "Suppose I do nothing. Suppose I don't respond to the COMPLAINT. Suppose I just pretend that nothing has happened."

"The court would issue a warrant for your arrest."

"And then?"

"Eventually, you'd be forced to stand trial."

"For what?"

"For failure to answer . . . and then for the million-seven-hundred-fifty-thousand-dollar lawsuit."

". . . Which Susskind could not possibly win."

"Well, if you're thinking of defending yourself, I'm not so sure. You know the old saying, 'A man who has himself for a lawyer has a fool for a client.' "

"A man who has a *lawyer* for a lawyer has a *pauper* for a client," I replied, straining at the ridiculous.

The truth was, I'd seriously considered doing nothing. I would hide someplace, if necessary. Get out of the state, whatever that amounted to legally. If Susskind persisted, and they finally caught up with me, I'd prepare counterclaims in obscure legal jargon of comparable absurdity to make mockery of the entire proceeding. I would become an irritant of such gothic proportions, I would make Susskind and his lawyers sick of the entire affair. And though it might stretch over many months, I would at least enjoy the process. There would be no great drain on my finances and the pleasure of the chase would spark my creative energies. I might even sell my notes to the *New York Law Journal!*

As Janet would put it: "I'll bring you some home-baked chocolate chip cookies in jail."

"I'm going overboard, eh?"

"You *do* have a tendency, you know."

Fortunately, there were sensible alternatives. It occurred to me that I might be able to dissuade Susskind and/or his attorneys through the good offices of two parties named in the COMPLAINT, viz., NBC and IBM. Through them, I would expose the total falsity of his case against me, thereby forcing him to drop the action.

How could he possibly continue to sue me when the very essence of his charges was summarily refuted by the executives involved?

I began by calling Bill Storke at NBC. When I told him that I was being sued, he seemed genuinely surprised. All the more so when I read him the paragraphs relating to my alleged dealings with NBC.

"Eliot, you said you would *not* sue. I remember your very words," he said. " 'I'm not the litigious type,' you told me." Precisely what I had hoped his response would be.

"Bill, if I could get a simple letter from you to that effect, it would be an enormous help . . ."

He explained—for all his sympathy for my plight—that he was terribly harassed at the moment, that he was leaving for Europe on a month's vacation that very day, that he really couldn't do anything about it right then. He asked that I call him on his return, just after the first of August.

I then called Chuck Francis at IBM. He was more than sympathetic; he was somewhat horrified. That such a travesty should result from this experience seemed terribly embarrassing.

Still, he was an executive at a large corporation. He wasn't quite sure as to what he could do to help me.

"Did you talk to Bill Storke?" he asked.

I replied that I had, and reported the indecisive outcome. I could almost see him shaking his head in dismay.

"I'll have to talk to the attorneys here," he said. "I don't see how I can get involved without consulting them." He promised to get back to me shortly.

A few days later, he did. He was deeply sorry, but he could not oblige my request for a statement. I reminded him that my efforts at this point might conceivably prevent a far greater involvement on his part in the future, what with lengthy depositions, possibly even testimony in court. "It seems to me that a simple letter specifying what took place that day might swing a lot of weight."

"I'm terribly sorry, Eliot."

I did not doubt him for a moment. Nor was I surprised when Bob Jagoda of IBM called later that week—a night call—to report that he'd heard about the lawsuit, that he thought it was a foul thing to have happened to me. He quickly explained that he was also in a difficult position ("I am not making this call, Eliot") but that I could count on him to back me up all the way. In the background, I could hear the sounds of the Democratic convention on his television, then his wife's voice nearer the phone. Bob laughed: "My wife said I got the courage to call you after listening to Cesar Chavez's speech."

Thank you, Cesar Chavez.

Then I'd visited with Robert Alan Aurthur, a man of many talents: novelist, playwright, television and film scenarist, monthly column writer for *Esquire* magazine, television producer. He was also an old friend. As a longtime intimate of Susskind (beginning over twenty years ago when Bob had written the triumphant "Mr. Peepers"), he was the perfect man to consult with. I would lay bare the problems, and he would supply the solutions. More, the way I saw it, he would march directly into Susskind's office and tell David that he was making a terrible mistake and get him to call off those dogs of his.

No doubt he had heard about the matter, but I made certain he heard all the nuances from my point of view. I sat in his marvelous home in East Hampton, Long Island, spinning the yarn all the way through, and when I stopped, I relaxed, prepared to enjoy his indignation.

"You deserve to be sued!"

"What!"

"It's your fault. You blew it."

At first I thought he was joking, his words seemed that incredible to me.

"You had no right to go to NBC and certainly not to the sponsor," he said.

"But what could I do? Susskind was taking over my book!"

"He offered to pay you for it. What else do you want? He didn't even have to do that. You don't own the Black Sox Scandal. It's public domain."

I wasn't about to go another long round with all my reasons, rehashing old questions.

"What would *you* have done, Bob?" I asked.

"I'd have gone straight to David and only to David."

"But I tried. I called him repeatedly . . ."

"Then you didn't try hard enough. You got sore at him, and that was a mistake you should never have made. A writer is not supposed to mess around with network people. A producer does that. And to go to the sponsor is absolutely unheard of."

"Maybe someone ought to write a guidebook . . ."

"David was simply taking a producer's stand in this issue. Any producer would do the same."

"Well, *you* wouldn't," I said. "If you were producing, you wouldn't go around corners as David did. It was damned devious . . ."

"If I had a deal with a network to produce a big show like this, I'd do whatever I had to do to get it on—as long as it was legal."

"And would you have sued me if you were in David's shoes?"

He didn't like the question, but he didn't back away from the answer.

"If I had to, yes . . ."

"You'd sue *me!*"

"You made too much of it. You should have taken the money. He had a million dollars riding on that show. No producer would let that slip by."

Well, this was Bob Aurthur with his producer's hat on, as they say. Also, I assumed, his friendship with David. Out of friendship with me, he proposed a possible solution.

"You want to get him to call off the suit? Go to him. Tell him you made a mistake. Sign the agreement so he can get the show on next season. That's the whole basis for the suit, El: he wants to force your hand."

"No," I said. "I won't do that. I'd rather sell the rights elsewhere!"

Bob shook his head as though I were making the biggest mistake of all. "Then you're probably doomed," he said.

It was not a particularly triumphant meeting.

The day after Bill Storke returned from his vacation, I was back in his office again. He read the COMPLAINT and sighed at the preposterous claims. And just as Chuck Francis had done, Storke replied that he would have to discuss this with NBC's counsel. As an executive, he could not take this on his own. Again, I advised him that any help he could give me now would be far more beneficial to himself and NBC as well as to me than what he might be compelled to do later. He understood that. He would call me.

He called two days later. Again, as with Francis, his reply was that the corporation's lawyers had advised him against doing any such thing.

I was continually going back to square one.

"This is beginning to make me very nervous," Janet said.

"What you need is a good job," I said.

"What *you* need is a good lawyer," she replied.

"My God, Janet, are you *that* nervous?"

"Aren't you?"

We carried on a considerable discussion as to how nervous I ought to be. The result was, I was now sitting in Ed Costikyan's office.

"It all boils down to costs," I told him. "The prospect of spending twenty-five thousand to win is really no different than losing the million, seven hundred and fifty thousand. I mean, I might just as well defend the action myself and lose!"

He understood that, too. As I said, he was sympathetic. He said he thought there would be a way to avoid trial.

"I'll see what I can do," he said.

So I left those distinguished offices feeling a lot better about my prospects. There was something terribly supportive about having Paul, Weiss, Rifkind, Wharton, & Garrison on one's side. I could even picture Hardee, Barovick, Konecky, & Braun receiving the first official reply from Costikyan and cowering at the sight of that letterhead.

(They used to say that Sandy Koufax beat a lot of ball clubs just by throwing his glove on the mound.)

Unfortunately, there was no cowering. One might even suggest that they simply braced themselves for a more formidable attack. Not even Costikyan's political power play (he'd tossed his hat in the ring as a candidate for mayor of New York) seemed to shake them up. I found that amusing (my lawyer, the mayor) though disconcerting (it was a pipe dream), wondering how he could justify handling so ludicrous a case as mine while he went battling for what had to be the most difficult political office in the history of civilization.

So nothing happened. The rival lawyers called each other, exchanged letters, then called each other again. The summer of 1976 ended in continuing irresolution. I was scheduled to be deposed on September 23, an appearance in Ron Konecky's office where I would be questioned in the presence of a court stenographer, an opening move in the preparation of their case. As it turned out, that date was adjourned for a month.

It was clear that Susskind had the initiative. Though we had discussed the possibility of a countersuit, Costikyan advised against it: for that, too, was likely to be expensive.

We held the defensive posture and waited.

I waited, but not patiently, playing with the thought that there had to be something I could do.

Like going to the press, for example.

27.

It was an idea I'd had from the inception of the lawsuit. That I did not implement it immediately was due primarily to my incredulity that Susskind would persist. Now, as I saw it, he was leaving me no choice. If the press would expose the story, it would surely be to my benefit. It might even embarrass him into submission. Though lawyers are inclined to oppose such extralegal tactics, especially during the course of negotiations, I had reached the point where I had to make a move.

I saw it as a magazine piece in *New York* magazine. Or *TV Guide*. Or a news story in *The New York Times*, or the *New York Post*. I began with the *Times*, quickly eliciting their interest. At the same time, a reporter for *Sports Illustrated* saw the potential story and interviewed me. There was also a lengthy phone conversation with an editor at *TV Guide*. I suggested that they contact Susskind himself for comment, my intent being to let him know that substantial coverage was in the offing.

Then John O'Connor, television critic of *The New York Times,* called. Would I consent to be interviewed about this matter? I eagerly accepted and visited him in his apartment the following afternoon.

What intrigued me was the theme that ran through all these interviews: an increasing resistance to television dramas that abused history. "Docudramas," they'd been labeled by the industry, but they leaned far more toward drama than documentation. It was immediately clear that this was O'Connor's main concern—as it was mine—and we spent a fascinating hour discussing what I felt was the Carrolls' script's distortion of history. A good interview, I thought, watching him work on his note pad as we talked. He would, of course, call Susskind for his reactions and comments, for which I could not have been more pleased. By now, I saw my counterattack assuming the proportions of a barrage.

Naturally, I reported all this to Ed Costikyan.

"God, no!" he cried out.

"What's wrong?"

"I just spoke with Konecky. Susskind wants to settle the case."

"Ha!" I cried out, proud of my tactic.

"You'd better call off the press," he said. "I don't think he'll appreciate all that publicity."

"But that's what made him decide to settle!" I argued.

"Get it stopped, Eliot. I'm right on the verge."

It was really too much. We were getting nowhere until I went to the press, and because I did, Susskind finally decided to quit. Now I was supposed to stop the story out of fear that he would be provoked into suing me again.

The way I saw it, O'Connor's article would work *for* me, not against me, for it would make it all the more difficult for Susskind to do anything with that script of his. And wasn't that now my principal motive?

"No," replied Costikyan. "You've got to get him to drop the suit. *That's* what we're after!"

In the end, I took his advice.

I called *TV Guide* and *Sports Illustrated* and asked them to stop work on the story. They agreed. I finally reached John O'Connor at Southampton, Long Island, but too late to pull his story, already scheduled for the coming Sunday "Arts and Leisure" section. O'Connor said he would call Susskind for a confirmation, and amend the story if necessary. On the following day, John called me back.

"It's true, all right," O'Connor said. "Susskind is withdrawing the suit. He told me: 'Asinof has his book, we have our script; we will proceed in our separate ways.'"

I could only wonder what that was supposed to mean.

O'Connor's article appeared on Sunday, October 24, 1976. "Blowing the Whistle on Dramatic License," it was headlined. ". . . American television's contempt for its raw material must be interpreted as contempt for its audience and, indeed, for the medium itself. The industry's dirty little secret is that many of the key executives responsible for content make a point of not watching their product beyond the launching stage. They are too busy, evidently, making noble speeches designed to generate and protect booming profits. Meanwhile, the general programming process, in its reckless rush toward the banal and the violent, becomes incredibly cheapening to all concerned. . . ."

O'Connor cited two current illustrations, one, the corruption of Taylor Caldwell's book *The Captains and the Kings* on a new NBC series, and the other, the project "Say It Ain't So, Joe," wherein "the writer of the book dealing with the subject had decided that 'there's a time when you finally have to say stop.'"

His piece capsulized the complex saga of my problems and my anger toward Susskind. Indeed, it would have to infuriate him.

It did. Less than a week later, Costikyan called to inform me that all negotiations had broken down as a result, both lawyers agreeing that it might be best to let Susskind have a cooling-off period.

"What about the October date for my deposition?" I asked.

"Adjourned," he replied. "We'll just have to sit it out for a while."

Why adjourned? I wondered. Why was Susskind neither pursuing nor terminating the case? Had I knocked his TV show out of the box with that newspaper piece? While I did not believe that for a moment, what actually *was* happening?

It had turned into a bloody war of nerves.

I suppose it was inevitable that this should begin to wear me down. I'd been under the legal gun for over four months now—not counting the turbulent year that had preceded the COMPLAINT—and hardly a day went by without some reference to it. It was like walking around with a shiner. Everybody I knew was aware of the case, and, out of concern, they would ask how it was going. Defensively, I would make jokes about it: "There's really no lawsuit. I'm just trying to help Ed Costikyan with the mayoralty nomination." Or, "The whole thing is a publicity stunt David Susskind dreamed up to promote his new film 'The Black Sox versus the Bad News Bears.'"

I even heard that my old Hollywood agent (whose potential sale of *Eight Men Out* to Twentieth Century-Fox in 1963 had been frustrated by the Dutch Ruether lawsuit) was in New York commenting that "to deal with Eliot Asinof was to take on a lawsuit."

For a person who avoided lawyers like the plague, I was becoming famous as a litigant.

"It's damn lucky you're not rich," said Janet.

For the first time in recent memory, I had to agree with that slant.

"It's my way of beating the system," I said.

As the great Leroy "Satchel" Paige had put it: "Don't look back. Something may be gaining on you!"

In midwinter 1977, there was more strange, upsetting news, though all part of the same old ball game:

Susskind was trying to reactivate the television project. Having failed to get the show on the air in 1976, he was shooting for a production in 1977.

News of this reached me from an inside source of unimpeachable reliability. A Deep Throat, as it were, whom I must refer to as X.

"This will really zap you," X reported in January. "Bill Storke is offering 'Say It Ain't So, Joe' for sale!"

I had barely reacted to the shock when X hit me with the double-whammy: "What's more, he says that IBM is interested! He says they're right on the brink of a deal, too. And they've got Red Smith to serve as 'technical advisor.' "

It was really too much. I called Bob Jagoda at IBM immediately. Had he heard any of this? Was it true?

Yes, a revised script had arrived for their scrutiny. And yes, he did hear Red Smith's name in connection with the project.

But no, IBM was definitely not interested.

I called Red at his home in Connecticut.

"Yes, one of the Carrolls called me. Then, Susskind himself. I really don't know what this is all about, Eliot . . ."

A few days later, Red and I met for lunch at Toots Shor's. He told me he had read the script but did not hold it in high regard.

"I told Susskind that I was not an expert on the Black Sox Scandal. All I knew about it was from the John Lardner piece in the old *Saturday Evening Post*, then your book. I was just a boy in Green Bay, Wisconsin, when it happened."

"Susskind wouldn't care if you never even heard of the Scandal," I said. "To the American people, you're the dean of sportswriters, Red. Your name associated with the script would make it respectable."

When I told him the whole history of the affair, he immediately became sympathetic. He said he wanted no part of such a tainted project. He would write Susskind a letter to so indicate.

"Did he offer you any money?" I asked.

"No. I guess we hadn't reached that point."

I told Red how much I appreciated his stand in this matter, especially since it would be at some financial sacrifice to himself.

But the very same week, X informed me that Diana Kerew, the original producer of 'Say It Ain't So, Joe,' reported that "the project had long since been dropped," then sent a copy of the newly revised script!

It was enough to confuse the balls off a brass monkey.

Nor did my reading of the so-called revised script make any sense. Now retitled "The Black Sox Scandal," precious little else had changed. A scene here, a line or two of dialogue there, hardly enough to retype a dozen pages. All the major inaccuracies prevailed.

Meanwhile, in light of all this renewed effort to revive the project, I was not surprised to hear that the lawyers were back in action.

There was, for example, a spirited call from Ed Costikyan:

"Well, I think we finally have a settlement!" he said. Konecky had offered terms for the termination of the suit: If I would desist from maligning the script and interfering with the sale and implementation of the project, TA would agree not to interfere with my rights to my book.

It was as John O'Connor had written quoting Susskind: "We have our script, and Asinof has his book."

I didn't know what to say.

"All it takes is your signature," Costikyan said. "I'll send you two copies."

They arrived in the mail on the following day. I read the proposed two-page agreement carefully. When Costikyan called again, I still didn't know what to say.

"Eliot, what's the trouble?" Ed asked. "Konecky keeps calling me. He is really annoyed. He advised me that unless you sign this agreement, they're going ahead with the suit!"

"But Susskind is still trying to do that show!" I replied. "He wants me to sit quietly and do nothing while he takes it away from me. Jesus, for him to abandon that 1960 claim as a trade for my complicity is like offering to swap an old skateboard for a new Mercedes."

It was, for all intents and purposes, the very same agreement he'd offered me $25,000 to sign!

"But you can't stop it anyway," Costikyan said. "You know that."

"Sure. But if I sign this, I can't even try!"

What continued to confuse me was Susskind's need for my signature. Why did he need any agreement with me if his right to produce his show was so legitimate? If the Carrolls' script was so great, how could I possibly continue to jeopardize his deal?

"Eliot, listen carefully." Costikyan took on new, more somber tones. "I know your feelings on this, but they're suing you! Now, you *know* what that might mean, the kind of money it might cost you, even to win. This would terminate the whole affair. I know it's not exactly what you want, but it's a workable compromise. You just can't expect them to give up completely . . ."

"I appreciate your advice, Ed. I'll think it over."

"Sign it, Eliot!"

"Well, here we are again," I shuddered.

"Where?" asked Janet.

"Back at good old square one."

"You look like you're drunk and don't know it."

"I think I'll have a drink," I said.

"I'm sick of square one," she began. "I'm sick of the whole damned business!"

"Who isn't?" I mumbled.

"I'll tell you something: I think maybe you are going bananas with it. I mean, what in hell are you going to do? Are you still thinking of *not* signing? Are you?"

The suddenness of her capitulation shocked me.

"I swear, I don't know."

"But that's so goddamn *dumb!*" Suddenly she was an injured tigress about this. I could even see the pain in her eyes, the ugly curl of her mouth. It was a moment when she couldn't have sung "Jingle Bells" even for a job at the Met. "Why can't you quit already? What more do you have to prove! I mean, Jesus, aren't you absolutely sick of it!"

I wanted to reply, but short of snapping back, I didn't know how. Besides, nothing I could say would stop her, anyway.

"Well, what *are* you going to do!"

Before I could even dissemble, she was on me again.

"If I know you, you're gonna tell him to go fuck himself. That's it, isn't it? *Isn't it?!*"

She was really shouting at me now, like one who wanted to pry a specific response out of me by the sheer power of her voice.

"No!" I shouted back, hating this. "I don't know!"

"You know what you remind me of? That crazy bird joke of yours." (The Kee-ri bird, known to fly in ever-decreasing concentric circles until it flies up its own asshole hollering "Kee-rist it's dark up here!")

She was glaring at me, shouting: "This is all such shit!" Then, with what I took to be three parts anger and two parts shame, she stalked out of the apartment.

Whatever it did for her, it was no help to me. I went to the door to bring her back, relying on the built-in cooling-off period until the elevator arrived, but she had disappeared, presumably opting to take the stairs rather than to stand there waiting.

Alone, I began to seethe. Unresolved arguments can be as frustrating as interrupted coitus. A man could choke on the words he didn't get a chance to say. My hand closed around the glass of Scotch as though it were Susskind's throat, and I let out a yell, some dumb, unspellable roar that wasn't even an obscenity. For all my rage, I set the drink down if only to avoid throwing it, wanting to prove to myself that I was in control. Indeed, I picked up Talent Associates' proffered letter of agreement with its preposterous quid pro quo and Costikyan's "Sign it, Eliot!" ringing in my ears. Another decision, another crisis. It was like being strapped in a dentist's chair as he kept drilling on the same damned tooth. The toughest war to fight is always the war of attrition. It was as if Susskind might get his way by boring me to death. Indeed, I could see all the blessings of capitulation. The end of shit, as Janet had put it. If there would be no happy ending, at least there would be an ending, and there was plenty to be said for that. No doubt I could make peace with it readily enough. I was, after all, a writer, at least part schmuck-with-typewriter, trained to eat shit as a compulsory ingredient in my diet.

It was painful. One suffers pain in waves, and my tolerance was definitely at ebb. This had been a time when I needed a victory, but there had been only rejection, enough to feed the paranoid sense that made all defeats seem inevitable—like the memory of a Hollywood jaunt barely a month before:

I had gone there hoping to make a television-film deal on the most intriguing sports biography I'd ever come across. It dealt with Ty Cobb's dying year as brilliantly portrayed by Al Stump, his biographer, wherein Cobb, an irascible bully of a man at seventy-three, showed the same ferocious qualities while resisting death that had made him the greatest ballplayer who ever lived, destroying every decent relationship he'd ever had because he did not want anyone to mourn for him. I wanted to expose this through his biographer's eyes, a young man living through an experience that began with fear and hatred, then ended with understanding and compassion. I spilled all this out in the executive offices of an old friend, now a power in television filmmaking. He listened politely enough, then began softening the characterization; he even put a woman in Cobb's life to hold his trembling hand, anything to make Cobb lovable, to coat the story with a bittersweetness. In the end, of course, he rejected it. What he really wanted was for me to get to Joe DiMaggio, to convince this most private person to sell himself for an intimate television special on his celebrated romance with Marilyn Monroe.

"Christ, Lou, that's shit!" I protested.

He shrugged, half agreeing, half not.

"Shit goes," he said, the ultimate Hollywood cliché to justify its perpetuation. The town was full of them; it needed them; the more insulting to the business, the more one heard them. "Underneath all the tinsel in Hollywood was the *real* tinsel"—that sort of thing. That a man like Lou should say it was a cliché in itself, for he had once been a highly promising playwright. No doubt they had hired him for his capacity to develop the best stories, and no doubt he was fully convinced that because of him the stories were better.

Better than what, I wondered.

Another writer I knew had pitched a story to him, a strong family drama with all the necessary conflicts, whereupon Lou had pronounced the last word in Hollywood rejections: "It's good, all right, but where's the shark?"

So now he wanted to include me. I was to solicit DiMaggio so that fifty million viewers might wallow in the bathos of his romance-of-the-decade. "Oh, it'd be sensational, Joe . . . Just think, you could even play yourself, show how you suffered when she dumped you for Arthur Miller. We could play a scene about the last time you had her in the sack: there's a big argument that builds to a terrific emotional, sexual climax where you screw her all over the apartment, and when it ends, we know you'll never forget her, never, no matter whom she marries. And the funeral scene, after she commits suicide—you're laying those flowers on her grave; it's your whole life right there, Joe, it might as well be you in that grave . . ."

Christ.

"What the hell," Lou was saying; "he shills for a bank, doesn't he."

Sure. There it was. There's always a justification for whatever you want to do; just find something rotten about your intended victim and then you can zap him without feeling guilty. The Godfather Ethic, I call it. Remember the key scene? There's old Marlon Brando/Don Corleone telling the five families that he won't submit to the narcotics trade, it's bad for the kiddies, it's even unpatriotic. He's so absolutely heroic, they have to try to kill him. What followed is perhaps the most brutal bloodbath ever filmed, but was there ever a greater justification? Didn't everyone feel absolutely *clean* as they rooted for it?

To my friend Lou, DiMaggio was expendable. If they could, they would take what was left of him. I thought of Joe, sitting at lunch in Gallagher's Steak House in New York, when a lady stopped by the table, recognizing him.

"Say, I know you," she said. "Aren't you the gentleman from the Bowery Savings Bank?"

He could handle Bob Feller, but he couldn't handle that lady.

And I, whom could I handle?

Obviously, not even myself. I had a sense of going under. I'd seen too many of us do that over the years. Since I'd been a ballplayer, it seemed as though America had suffered a sickening history of shocks to its system—like reading in 1947 that there were fourteen thousand new American millionaires as a result of World War II. Then McCarthyism, Vietnam, Nixon, Watergate. And all the while, a generation and more had been facing the first full flush of television with its concomitant flood of advertising. It was the age of the relentless hype. So much shit was being thrown around, inevitably it came to be acceptable. "Shit goes," the Hollywood man had said, and the rest of us learned to eat it, even to justify the eating by pretending it wasn't shit at all. If, as it has been said, my generation had "sold out" to this monstrosity, what followed us was a generation who "bought in." Inevitably, then, there were those who would even sell out what they had bought into. We had become an affluence of leeches, wheeler-dealers, hustlers, brokers, manipulators—some legal, some not. It didn't matter; the goal was for the same big bucks.

Would Joe DiMaggio have done commercials a generation ago? Or, more significantly, does anyone think badly of it today?

Indeed, who can escape the power of this onslaught? In the world of the so-called arts, are there any survivors? Was there ever a more talented, more exciting, more *commercial* actor than Marlon?

They took his individuality and labeled him a "rebel," then packaged and merchandised it until it became chic. I watched him wrestle with these manipulations during the early years of his brilliance. In defiance, he tried to make his own films, but he was an actor not a filmmaker and certainly not a businessman. There was too much pressure on him, too much money at stake. And then, after a spate of failures, there was much too little.

To those who respected him, his demise seemed incredible. But the final irony was that he should make his comeback in *The Godfather*—an Oscar for his glorification of the ultimate symbol of our decadence.

He didn't want it to be that way. Otherwise, he would not have put on a hundred pounds.

"Sign the agreement, Eliot!" said Costikyan.

Those eight guys, the so-called Black Sox who sold out the 1919 World Series . . . they'd been cheated and abused and exploited. They'd seen gamblers run through the baseball establishment without anyone laying a glove on them. If throwing the World Series was a heinous act, the way they saw it, they were only getting even.

One could practically say that the excuse for the Black Sox Scandal itself had become the excuse for selling out my book, for it would only be doing to the ballplayers what they did to baseball!

The phone rang, and I answered with exaggerated brusqueness. It was Janet.

"I'm sorry," she said, her voice as soft as silk.

"It's okay."

"I just wanted you to know."

"Okay, I know."

"But I'm not coming back until after you decide."

It seemed sensible enough. She didn't want to pressure me. Besides, I remembered that she had an audition for a deodorant commercial in the morning.

Costikyan called early the next day.

"They want your signature, Eliot."

"You mean they called you again, so early?"

"It's only the beginning," he said.

It amused me. What could demand such urgency? Had Susskind really taken his production to the brink of some new deal, wherein the threat of another beef from me could intimidate him? Did he really need that piece of paper with my acquiescence?

It didn't matter. I had made up my mind. I delivered my well-rehearsed message in the most precise legal terminology:

"Ed, tell them to go fuck themselves."

He sighed, not with relief but with pain.

I told him that he should send me a bill, that I was grateful for all his efforts.

"Good luck," he said.

It sounded like a dirge.

Later, I stopped in at Janet's restaurant to deliver the news. She was not upset. In fact, I sensed a touch of relief.

"What happened at your audition?" I asked.

"I didn't go," she said.

"What! Why not?"

She shrugged, started to reply, then shook it off with a smile.

"Fuck 'em all, big and small," she said.

It was hardly a week after I said good-bye to Ed Costikyan that I received the following letter:

Please be advised that pursuant to the Notice of Deposition dated August 5, 1976, the deposition of Eliot Asinof is hereby scheduled for Wednesday, February 23, 1977, at 10:00 at our offices.

> Very truly yours,
> Hardee, Barovick, Konecky
> & Braun
> [signed] Stephen Ross

Well, there it was. After seven months of dallying, the call to combat had finally been sounded, and I was totally without professional defense.

A bit frightening, to be sure. It was one thing to have rattled my saber from the safety of a living room; it was quite another to contend with the enemy on the battlefield.

Frightening, and in this instance, confusing as well.

Barely a few days after Ross's letter, X informed me that Bill Storke had remarked at NBC that the Black Sox project was "once again in serious legal difficulties," but according to Red Smith, "Susskind told me there was really no such lawsuit at all!"

I remembered a scene on a television show wherein the eighty-year-old Groucho Marx, sitting on the fringes of a large party, saw a midget in cutaways, replete with cigar, heavy eyebrows, glasses, Marxian mustache, and that familiar Groucho walk.

"Who are *you?*" Groucho asked.

"I'm Groucho Marx," the midget replied.

Groucho looked stunned for a moment, then, with typical disdain, sent him on his way. "Go mingle, will you," Groucho said, "Then come back and tell me if I'm having a good time."

My problem was to find a new lawyer to defend a $1,750,000 lawsuit that the plaintiff said does not exist.

To begin with, I had to get the date of the deposition postponed. I called Stephen Ross, the new attorney assigned to the case at Hardee, Barovick, Konecky, & Braun, and so requested.

"Give me two weeks to get a new attorney," I asked.

He said, "All right, two weeks," then called back the same afternoon to reverse himself. Indignantly, I wrote him a certified letter saying that I would simply not be present for the deposition on the twenty-third, reminding him that twice previously his office had set dates at which I was prepared to attend—which *they* chose to adjourn.

Lawyer, lawyer, who's got a lawyer?

Everybody, of course, for lawyers are as plentiful as automobile repairmen. I had vague notions of finding some recent graduate of law school who had passed his bar exams. I had even spoken with the dean of Columbia Law School, seeking his recommendations. (He refused to participate in such "an irresponsible procedure.") I called a number of friends with less-than-promising results, then took to fingering through the Yellow Pages in hopes of coming upon some familiar but long-forgotten name. It was, admittedly, not the healthiest of situations, and I was liking it less and less.

Then, out of the blue, my morning mail included an announcement that Joel V. Braziller, attorney at law, was entering private practice and could be reached at his home in Brooklyn Heights.

Joel, known to me as Jim, was the son of George Braziller, distinguished publisher, friend, fellow golfer. I had known Jim for a half-dozen years when he was counsel for a New York state environmental-protection agency. He was bright, high-minded, and eager—and was in no position to demand exorbitant fees.

"You're crazy!" friends shouted at me. "Would you let a young surgeon make his first operation on you?"

"Why not, if he let me tell him where to cut."

By now, I had a whole new scenario worked out in my head, a compromised version of hiring myself as a lawyer. By this time, I'd been playing the law game long enough to know a few of its wrinkles. Besides, I'd seen a few old pros at work and talked to others; they all conceded that, in this case, very little actual knowledge of the law was involved. Was not TA vs. Asinof more a simple power play than a game of chess? The thing to do, then, was to abandon a defensive posture and go on the attack. Instead of warding off their random blows, we'd strike back and take their game away from them.

It was precisely the sort of tactic a young lawyer might enjoy getting his feet wet on. As I saw it, it might be fun for a change. And who knows; it might even work.

Not having an office in Manhattan, Jim was willing to make house calls—which put me ahead of the game from the opening whistle. We had a three-hour consultation in my apartment. He took over all the documents, from the COMPLAINT of the previous June (1976) through all the correspondence of the previous attorneys. He also insisted on reading my book and the Sidney Carroll script.

In one day, he had broken all known precedent as counselor.

After arranging a two-week postponement of the deposition, we worked up a bill of particulars in which Susskind was challenged to show cause for every item in the COMPLAINT. If I had maliciously defamed Susskind and the Carrolls and TA, to whom had I done it, and how, and when? If I had threatened lawsuit, or claimed infringement of copyright, that, too, must be explained. In addition, we filed a countersuit against Susskind for damaging *my* equity by falsely claiming ownership of the rights, and demanded damages of $300,000.

If nothing else, we would drown the bastards in paperwork.

In the midst of this, it should surprise no one that the Hollywood trade papers again announced the pending production of a television show called "Say It Ain't So, Joe." This one was to be produced at Columbia Pictures Television by Frank Telford, script by Elliot Roberts, both of whom were reputable, well-established Hollywood professionals.

More bees around the honeycomb.

So I was back on the phone again, this time to Larry White, head of the studio allegedly involved.

I told him of the Telford announcement in the trades. Was Screen Gems actually in production? He went over his list of projects in work, but had no record of it. This was not extraordinary, he advised me, for it could be one of many projects for which there was, as yet, no commitment. Or, more likely, a phony announcement to drum up publicity.

He promised to check it out.

A few days later, a call came in from René Valente, another executive at Columbia Pictures Television. She, too, was an old friend. (She used to work for David Susskind.)

"There *is* a script," she told me. "No mention of your book. Apparently, it's a patchwork job based on newspaper clippings."

"Sounds nasty," I said.

"Don't worry, we're turning it down," she replied. "You don't think we'd do anything about the Black Sox Scandal without calling you, do you!"

That was extremely nice to hear.

Then, on March 9, 1977, at long last, the deposition, the opening wedge in their preparation for trial. I was ready, for the way I saw it, Susskind and his attorneys would finally have to face my interpretation of the facts.

Steve Ross was young but experienced. He wore the dark, conservative suit of an establishment lawyer, and his manner bespoke courtesy and professionalism like one who had been doing this all his life.

Though I was prepared to assume an adversary posture, Ross quickly disabused me of it. He seemed totally impartial as he began the questioning, the ultimate fact-finder, as it were, respecting my version of even the most damaging testimony. I even found myself pulling back at times, wary of being trapped as I plunged into the holes he opened up for me. Over a span of several hours, he established my expertise in the Black Sox Scandal, the nature of my objections to the Carroll script, the purpose and scope of my protest to Bill Storke at NBC, the cause and effect of my meetings at IBM.

When we left, Jim and I agreed that it had been an extremely successful session. It really did not seem possible that they could pursue a case wherein all the stipulations of the COMPLAINT had just been blown apart.

"So, now what?" I asked.

"For the moment, nothing. We wait to see what moves they choose to make."

"Then it's our turn?"

"Right. We depose Storke, then Chuck Francis of IBM . . ."

I could envision the success of such depositions and what would have to be their impact on Susskind's suit. I could also see a lot of my money go fluttering away in the process, for the cost of the court stenographer alone was enough to build a fair-sized battleship.

But I no longer cared about the money. I liked the feel of the way the cookie was crumbling. In lighter moments, I would play out all the usual fantasies about the oncoming trial. I'd be a man under the gun for almost $2,000,000, but you'd never know it. I'd be as insouciant as Cary Grant on the best day he ever had. I'd take on every lawyer they had, reply to every question without a moment's hesitation, repeat the truth in the face of every entrapment however artful, maintain my poise though they call my mother a whore and my son a rapist. I'd win, all right, and it wouldn't matter that I'd win nothing but the victory, that in fact I'd blown $25,000 and whatever else it might cost me. The point was, I wouldn't be just another schmuck-with-a-typewriter, would I? . . .

I became so surfeited with this enticing fantasy, it left me vulnerable to its reversal, and all that took was one flash of foreboding:

"Suppose, just suppose," it was suggested to me, "some of those big boys you're so eager to depose don't see the story quite the way you see it . . ."

That was enough. I could feel the chill of death in my bones. From such speculations, any normal paranoid could put the pieces of his doom together. After all, they were corporate executives, weren't they? And who could deny the effectiveness of any sharp lawyer at the first signs of doubt? Indeed, how many times had I written precisely that scene?

Add to that, these crushing words: "You really don't think Susskind and his lawyers would wittingly go into court with a case they couldn't win, do you?"

No, I guess I didn't.

End of fantasy. (I *never* fantasize on defeat.)

Then, a week later, Jim called again.

"Steve Ross just called me. He wants a postponement on their reply to our bill of particulars and countersuit."

"Don't give it to them!" I snapped.

"I suggest you hear their reason before you decide," he said, a twinkle in his voice that immediately moderated my venom.

"Okay. I'm listening."

"He tells me that Susskind is ready to throw in the towel."

Silence. I couldn't believe it. Not really.

"What? Without any conditions? Without a compromise of some sort?"

"That's the way it looks."

"Well, I'll be damned!" I cried out.

I still didn't believe it.

How could I? Even though it made sense, there was nothing in the scenario that prepared me for it. Everything had indicated a long, drawn-out battle to wear me down—a siege of attrition on my dwindling resources, tactical if not actually vindictive. This switch was too sudden to be credible. I felt like the prisoner on death row, already strapped into the electric chair, when the governor's call comes in to stay the execution. Better yet, this was not a reprieve or even a pardon: this was tantamount to full exoneration.

The trouble was, it takes a very special adjustment to cope with good news after you've learned to live with the bad. You tell yourself the glowing truth, but it doesn't take; it slides off the oily surface of your pessimism; you have to relearn the art of happy endings.

Janet, however, was prepared. She even had a bottle of Asti Spumanti hidden behind the carrots and celery in the fridge.

"You know something?" she said. "There was never a doubt."

I opened the bubbly wine with an equally bubbly burst of laughter.

"Well, hardly ever," I said.

"You fought the good fight," she said. "You showed the courage of the wounded lion."

"Right."

"And you licked him."

"I did, I did."

"The most sonovabitchin' thing I ever saw!"

"That it was."

"What's more, you beat the Mummy's Curse!"

"You shouldn't've said *that*," I said.

We celebrated with dinner at Orsini's, followed by too many drinks at too many wateringholes.

"What's gonna happen now?" Janet asked.

It was as if we had just lost a cantankerous old friend.

It took another month of legal doodling before the papers came through. Jim appeared in my apartment, and we laughed all the way to the notary public, where I affixed my signature to the final papers.

Susskind would drop his suit against me, and I would drop my countersuit against him.

There were absolutely no other conditions.

Now, *that* was what I'd call a proper quid pro quo.

And so it ended, May 9, 1977, twenty-seven months after I'd first sat in Susskind's office explaining the problem over rights— almost a year and a half after I'd first called Bill Storke at NBC.

We had won a total victory.

I took the rest of the day off.

30.

Throughout the spring, having sold the option on *The Fox Is Crazy Too,* I was hard at work on the screenplay, gradually reaching that point of satisfaction wherein I could pretend that De Niro or Redford, Nicholson or Pacino would leap at the chance to play the role. Such a film, with its accompanying screen credit, was the sort of thing that could change a writer's life, from nickels and dimes to big bucks. Besides, Holt, Rinehart and Winston was reissuing *Eight Men Out* in hardcover, fourteen years after its original publication—no small tribute to the life of that book.

This was definitely going to be my year, by God.

Then a phone call from Los Angeles hit me like the sting of a hornet. An actor friend, Ed Lauter, was on the line.

"Eliot, I thought you'd like to know," he began. "I just got a call for casting—a television film called 'Say It Ain't So, Joe.' "

"Christ!" I almost dropped the phone. "Who's involved this time?"

"Well, the director is Delbert Mann. The producer is Fred Brogger . . ."

"Stop!" I cried out. It was the same old Susskind crew, all right.

"They told me they were planning to shoot in August . . ."

Which probably meant a 1978 spring date for airing. They would show it to greet the opening of the baseball season.

Since X had left town for greener pastures, and was unreachable at the time, I could learn no further specifics. It took me two weeks to find out that NBC was no longer involved, that the production was to be financed by CBS. Then, almost immediately, X called from California to inform me that CBS had withdrawn its affiliation with the project.

"Great!" I said. "How come?"

"Well, one CBS executive called the script 'a piece of shit.' "

Ha, ha. That nifty little turn of phrase again. I could only wonder if Susskind would sue CBS for defaming his product and destroying his equity. After all, the words were exactly the same, weren't they? It was a beautiful postscript to my victory, adding poetry to justice. It was also the sort of pithy judgment that would bury Susskind's project once and for all.

As they say in Hollywood: You couldn't write it any better.

I should have known better. One would think that after all the twists and turns, after all the victories and reversals and the ups and downs, I would have guessed that the final flip would turn into a flop, that paranoia was indeed justified when all those forces out there were plotting against you.

Besides, there's that business about the curse being on the book, on the Black Sox, on me. Right?

But I didn't know. Not that it would have mattered except, perhaps, to mitigate that final shock. It was as if a big gambler left the ball park in the eighth inning, secure in the 7–0 lead he had, only to hear later that the opposition scored eight runs in the ninth. It can really stun you.

What happened was that Susskind and his company were bought up by Time Inc., and with the power and money of Time Inc. behind him, he was finally going into production.

That this grotesque piece of news should be delivered to me by a motion-picture producer who was eager to make the real *Eight Men Out* seemed altogether fitting.

"This makes this very difficult, you realize . . ." he said.

I realized, all right. It was highly unlikely that any studio would put up the millions to make a feature film of a story already slated to be shown on television—certainly not when the subject was as special as the Black Sox Scandal. Good, bad, or indifferent, it did not matter. Such a property immediately became a poor investment.

There were now *nine* men out.

How could it be that I'd won all the battles and lost the war?

How could such a thing have possibly happened!

For days, I went around red-eyed, spitting fire, cauldrons boiling in my gut. I hit concrete walls with white-knuckled fists, crashed through plate-glass windows, leaped off towering rooftops while immolated in flaming kerosene, but there was no surcease from my rage. What hurt was less the defeat itself than the startling, stabbing, slashing, skewering awareness of my idiocy: the truth was, I hadn't ever won a victory. Susskind had merely let me play with myself for a while then slapped my hand away with this latest coup. It was all a madness on my part. The whole fight had been a madness. Everything I had done had been a waste; the entire struggle was a total waste, for nothing I did or could have done would have stopped him from making this film. In all those maxi- and mini-crises, no matter what decision I had made, *it did not matter*. He knew he was going to beat me. He knew it all along.

Ha, ha, laughed the man who served me the COMPLAINT.

As it turned out, my rage did not diminish with time but drove me to purge myself in this telling of it. This, too, is a writer's right, not only to purge the defeat but to share it with the great fellowship of shit eaters. You win some, you lose some, as losers are wont to say, but there must be no dropping of the cudgel.

Of course, when you take on a situation such as this—with its mad tilting at imaginary windmills—you have to figure it's all a joke. You relegate it to a corner pocket of your brain reserved for absurdities, as a protection against the onslaught of too much frustration. It would have to be that way, I suppose, or we'd all go crazy. The joke, as everybody knows, is that history insists on repeating itself even with those who are fully able to understand it.

Take my ringing doorbell again, for example. It's almost exactly two years after the COMPLAINT. It's the mailman, this time, delivering a certified letter into my hot little hands. In the upper left-hand corner of the envelope, I see the all-too-familiar names of Hardee, Barovick, Konecky, & Braun. Susskind's lawyers, one and all. I will be excused a fresh attack of the shudders.

The letter, signed by Ron Konecky, is to warn me that David Susskind has heard of this book, that it is a defamatory collage of distortions, that unless I clear its content with him, both I and my publisher will be held liable for any and all damages.

Say, $1,750,000?